TRIALS
THANKS A LOT!

LORRAINE HOLMAN

TRIALS
THANKS A LOT!

TATE PUBLISHING & Enterprises

Published by Tate Publishing & Enterprises, LLC
127 E. Trade Center Terrace | Mustang, Oklahoma 73064 USA
1.888.361.9473 | www.tatepublishing.com

Tate Publishing is committed to excellence in the publishing industry. The company reflects the philosophy established by the founders, based on Psalm 68:11,
"The Lord gave the word and great was the company of those who published it."

Book design copyright © 2010 by Tate Publishing, LLC. All rights reserved.
Cover design by Tyler Evans
Interior design by Stephanie Woloszyn

Published in the United States of America

ISBN: 978-1-61663-308-0
1. Self-help / Motivational & Inspirational
2. Religion / Christian Life / Spiritual Growth
10.04.21

WITH THANKFUL APPRECIATION

Thank you, Lord—for saving, guiding, teaching, loving, correcting, blessing, and transforming me by your merciful hand. I am lost without you.

Thank you, Buddy—for fulfilling every dream I had of being completely loved by Mr. Right. I can't wait to spend another thirty years with you.

Thank you, Andy and Sarah Jane—for swelling my heart with love, pride, and joy simply because you call me Momma. I adored you as children, and now I admire you as adults. Thank you for allowing me to tell your stories.

Thank you, Dusty and Courtney—for loving my children. I'm thankful for the privilege of loving you as you've become a part of our family.

Thank you, Daddy and Momma—for laying a firm foundation in our family and supporting me with love and affirmation. Your marriage and parenting have been inspirational.

Thank you, Sadie Jane, Lily Grace, and all the grandbabies to come—for the amazing feelings that stir in me every time I see your precious little faces and hear the words "Ma Raine." We'll have great fun together!

Thank you, Sissy, Colleen, and Kim—for keeping me humble as only sisters can. I love you and am thankful you're always just a phone call away.

TABLE OF CONTENTS

PART TWO: MY TRIALS AND WHY I'M THANKFUL FOR THEM 115

INTRODUCTION

I accepted Jesus as my Lord and Savior at age thirteen, during the "Jesus Movement" of the 1970s. In our little Oklahoma church, we sang two popular Andrae Crouch songs, "My Tribute" and "Through It All." I remember singing my heart out and crying to these touching lyrics from "My Tribute":

> How can I say thanks for the things you have done for me?
> Things so undeserved, yet you give to prove your love for me.
> The voices of a million angels, cannot express my gratitude,
> All that I am or ever hope to be I owe it all to thee!

And from "Through It All":

> Through it all, through it all,
> I've learned to trust in Jesus—I've learned to trust in God.
> Through it all—through it all,
> I've learned to depend upon his word.
> I thank God for the mountains, and I thank him for the valleys,
> And I thank him for the storms he's brought me through,
> For if I never had a problem, I wouldn't know that he could solve them,
> I'd never know what faith in God could do.

Looking back, at the innocent and tender age of thirteen, I didn't have a clue what those lyrics meant. Oh, I was thankful for my salvation and the presence of God in my life, but my young faith had never been tested beyond being called a goody two-shoes at school!

I had no idea what God wanted to do with my life or what paths he had planned for me to walk.

Thirty-plus years later, these song lyrics speak to a deep well within my soul and cause gratitude and thanksgiving to pour out of my heart to my Lord, for he has seen me *through it all.* Not only has he seen me *through,* but also in each trial, he's made me a better person ("All that I am or ever hope to me, I owe it all to thee!").

If a Christian is defined as "one who is like Christ," then Christ-likeness is my life's goal. Without trials in my life, I'm certain I would never resemble Christ in any way, shape, or form. I still have a long way to go on this journey to Christlikeness, but oh, how far God has brought me already!

This book is a series of stories from my life. Each story is about a trial or trouble of some sort. The stories tell about days of aggravation, fear, hardship, and sorrow. With the benefit of 20/20 hindsight, I reflect on those difficulties and thank God for allowing each one in my life. Is that a shocking statement for you to hear? Believe me, I've seen many eyebrows raised when I've said I was *thankful* for the things I've been through! My prayer is that you may be able to relate to my stories and take a fresh look at your own trials—see them with fresh insight—and be thankful.

There's no doubt that my trials are small compared to the heartaches and burdens that others have endured. In no way do I claim to have had a life of turmoil. In fact, the opposite is true. I've lived a very blessed, happy, and relatively smooth life. My parents are still alive and happily married. I've been married over thirty years to my cutie-pie husband, Buddy, and I'm still crazy in love with him. I've never been unloved or abused. And I've never faced the death of an immediate family member. At this point, you may think I'm totally unqualified to speak about trials. But I hope that even the person who has faced the most tragic of trials would lend me an ear as I recount what I've learned in my light afflictions. My prayer is that the soul who sees his trial as the most unbearable of all can still glean perspective from the lessons I've learned. Perhaps God will use my little stories to help a hurting heart find something to be thankful for—even in the darkest of days.

FIRST THINGS FIRST

This book is unashamedly written from a Christian worldview. If you have never accepted Jesus as your personal Lord and Savior, let me encourage you to do so now. Believing that Jesus is the Son of God and born of a virgin is not considered being "born again." Even the demons in hell *believe* in Jesus, but they aren't spending eternity with him in heaven! The way to salvation is simple, but does require a bit more than just believing.

The first thing you must do to be saved is recognize that you are a sinner.

> For all have sinned and fall short of the glory of God.
>
> Romans 3:23

The next step is to realize that the penalty for your sin is eternal death, spent in hell and separated from God. But our merciful God has a plan that will save you from that eternal death, and it is an absolutely free gift to those who accept it. You can't be good enough to earn it or work hard enough to keep it; it is a gift.

> For the wages of sin is death, but the gift of God is eternal life in Christ Jesus our Lord.
>
> Romans 6:23

This next verse explains how God showed his great love for you by having his own son die for you while you were still a sinner. In other words, you didn't have to stop sinning for God to love you or for the innocent Christ to pay the price for your sins—he loved you in your sinful condition.

> But God demonstrates His own love toward us, in that while we were still sinners, Christ died for us.
>
> Romans 5:8

Now take a look at a verse that tells how you can accept this free gift of salvation.

> That if you confess with your mouth the Lord Jesus and believe in your heart that God has raised Him from the dead, you will be saved. For with the heart one believes to righteousness, and with the mouth confession is made to salvation.
>
> Romans 10:9–10

How amazingly simple God has made salvation for you! Simply believe and confess. Here's an example of a prayer that you might pray for salvation. Saying the exact words are not important; having the right heart attitude is.

> Lord, I know I am a sinner, and I'm sorry for the sins I've committed. I believe and confess that Jesus is the Son of God, and I believe that God raised him from the dead after he died for my sins. I ask you to forgive me, save me, and come live inside me as the Lord of my life. Thank you, Lord, and help me to live for you. In Jesus' name I pray, amen.

You might think this is way too easy. You may think that you have sinned too much and God cannot or will not save you. But the invitation is to *all*.

> For whoever calls upon the name of the Lord shall be saved.
>
> Romans 10:13

> If we confess our sins, He is faithful and just to forgive us our sins
> and to cleanse us from all unrighteousness.
>
> 1 John 1:9

If you've believed, if you've prayed a prayer similar to the one above, and if you've confessed it with your mouth, you have been saved! Jesus has become your personal Savior, he lives within you, and you are delivered from eternal death!

I encourage you to read the Bible and find a Bible-believing church to attend regularly. Just as little children need adults to teach them, brand-new Christians need mature Christians to help them grow spiritually.

If you expect to find perfect people in a church, you'll be disappointed. You should, however, find people who love the Lord and who will love you. You should look for a church whose members study the Bible and never compromise its teachings. Look for a church that reaches out to its community and isn't afraid to stand for righteousness. Look for a church where people will give you a warm welcome and together you can all work in the kingdom of God as he directs you. Your life will never be the same!

THANKSGIVING

◆

NOT JUST FOR NOVEMBER

O give thanks to the Lord, for He is good! For His mercy endures forever.

Psalm 107:1

Autumn leaves are gently falling down, the kitchen air smells of pumpkin pie baking in the oven, and you're mindful of the Pilgrims' journey across the ocean in the *Mayflower* in search of religious freedom. It must be Thanksgiving. It's the day our nation has set aside to be *thankful* to Almighty God for his goodness and provision to us. At least, that's what it's *supposed* to be about. Instead, it's the official kick off of the "holiday" shopping season—it's not politically correct to say *Christmas* anymore. Instead of being thankful on this holiday, we complain about how busy the season is, how we don't have time to cook, and how we would rather not spend the afternoon with relatives that get on our nerves while men sleep through football games they claim to be watching!

The Thanksgiving holiday only comes once a year, and even some Christians do a pitiful job at being thankful on that day. I confess that I've been guilty of putting more effort into making a perfect holiday rather than making a perfect heart with sincere thanksgiving to God. Let's take a look into God's Word and see if thanksgiving matters to him.

> All Scripture is given by inspiration of God, and is profitable for doctrine, for reproof, for correction, for instruction in righteousness, that the man of God may be complete, thoroughly equipped for every good work.
>
> 2 Timothy 3:16–17

If you believe the above scripture, which says that God inspires *all* Scripture, then you must recognize that everything in the Bible is there for a reason. What may seem like an insignificant detail to you and me is actually a detail that God thought was important enough to breathe into his recorded Word. Knowing this, let's take a look at Nehemiah 12.

> Moreover the Levites were Jeshua, Binnuei, Kadmiel, Sherebiah, Judah, and Mattaniah who led the thanksgiving psalms, he and his brethren.
>
> Nehemiah 12:8

Nehemiah led the children of Israel in rebuilding the city wall of Jerusalem after the Babylonians destroyed it. We read in Nehemiah 12 that the wall is complete, and the Israelites celebrate that completion and dedicate the wall. The entire chapter is filled with a long, long list of names of priests and Levites—which are all much too difficult for this Okie girl to pronounce. Right in the middle of this long list of names is a man named Mattaniah. He is one of the few men mentioned with a description—most names are simply listed with no other details given. But Mattaniah was noted because he led the thanksgiving psalms. We must assume this detail is important to God because he breathed it into Scripture. Six more times in this chapter alone, Scripture records *thanks* or *thanksgiving* as the people dedicated the city wall.

We need to understand what made these people so thankful about a new city wall. This day of thanksgiving and celebration took place after God's people had spent seventy years as captives in the faraway pagan land of Babylon. Upon their release from captivity, they made the long, difficult journey back home to Jerusalem—only to find it in utter ruin. The rebuilding effort was intense, and workers were required to wear weapons due to threats from their enemies, who were trying to prevent the rebuilding. With the wall finally completed, the city could now protect itself from its enemies. At last, God's people were home, in their own land, and for the first time in most of their lives, felt safe and free. What a day to be thankful!

A priest named Ezra read the Book of the Law to the people gathered that day—and they respectfully stood for hours while he read it. Upon hearing the Law, they wept when they realized they had been living in severe disobedience to the Lord. The people confessed their sin and returned to a right relationship with God. It was at this point—after the trials and heartaches they had endured for decades—that they dedicated the city wall with thankfulness.

> Now at the dedication of the wall of Jerusalem they sought out the Levites in all their places, to bring them to Jerusalem to celebrate the dedication with gladness, both with thanksgivings and singing, with cymbals and stringed instruments and harps.
>
> Nehemiah 12:27

When you look over your life at the list of trials you have faced, can you still be thankful to the Lord? Are you thankful for where you are and what you have? Are you thankful because God walked with you through the tough times? Or do you focus more on what you've lost or been cheated out of or how you've been hurt? Look around, dear one, and you'll find there is so much to be thankful for.

Even when we think our own particular situation is much too upsetting to give thanks for, God still instructs us to be thankful. No matter how good or how bad our circumstances may be, thanksgiving is an attitude God expects us to exhibit.

> And let the peace of God rule in your hearts, to which also you were called in one body; and be thankful.
>
> Colossians 3:15

> Rejoice always, pray without ceasing, in everything give thanks; for this is the will of God in Christ Jesus for you.
>
> 1 Thessalonians 5:16–18

> And do not be drunk with wine, in which is dissipation; but be filled with the Spirit, speaking to one another in psalms and hymns and spiritual songs, singing and making melody in your heart to the Lord, giving thanks always for all things to God the Father in the name of our Lord Jesus Christ, submitting to one another in the fear of God.
>
> Ephesians 5:18–21

How could anyone argue with the passages listed above? Over and over in the Bible, God's people are admonished to be thankful. And if we refuse to be thankful, there will be serious consequences.

> For since the creation of the world His invisible attributes are clearly seen, being understood by the things that are made, even His eternal power and God-head, so that they are without excuse, because, although they knew God, they did not glorify Him as God, nor were thankful, but became futile in their thoughts and their foolish hearts were darkened.
>
> Romans 1:20, 21

This passage basically says that there is no excuse for ignoring God—and that includes not being thankful to him. Further, we can see that this kind of person—one who ignores God and refuses to be thankful—will eventually find himself in a worrisome state, having his heart darkened.

You may be thinking right now that in *your* pain and *your* circumstances there cannot possibly be anything to be thankful for. In that case, may I suggest to your grieving heart that you start with one simple thought? Be thankful that you are loved.

> We love Him because He first loved us.
>
> 1 John 4:19

> The Lord has appeared of old to me, saying: "Yes, I have loved you with an everlasting love; therefore with lovingkindness I have drawn you."
>
> Jeremiah 31:3

> How precious is Your lovingkindness, O God! Therefore the children of men put their trust under the shadow of Your wings.
>
> Psalm 36:7

> Can a woman forget her nursing child, and not have compassion on the son of her womb? Surely they may forget, yet I will not forget you. See, I have inscribed you on the palms of My hands.
>
> Isaiah 49:15–16

Whether you feel loved or not, the fact remains: you are loved. Whether you believe it or doubt it, the fact remains: you are loved. Whether you understand it or not, the fact remains: you are loved. Whether you accept it or not, the fact remains: you are loved.

Yes, indeed, the God of this universe loves you. No matter how much pain you are in, no matter how awful your circumstances are, no matter how abandoned you are or how hopeless you feel, you are loved. No matter how many times you've failed him or what horrible sin you have committed, you are loved. You can be thankful that God always has and always will love you, no matter what. He loved you enough to sacrifice his only Son for you. It's a love you cannot measure or comprehend, but you, dear soul, are loved. Believe it and accept it. He loved you first, he has drawn you to himself, you're safe under the shadow of his wings, and he'll never forget you because your name is carved in his hands. Keep this one simple yet staggering thought in your mind: you are loved—and for that you can be thankful.

PART ONE:
WHY TRIALS COME

WHY ME, LORD?

In the midst of hard times, people always ask the same questions: "Why do trials come my way?" or "Why did a good God let that happen to me?" or "What did I do to deserve this?" I think these are valid questions, and I believe they should be addressed in any book that discusses trials. I do not claim to be a theologian, and certainly others are more qualified to address these questions than I am, but let's look into the Word of God and allow the Holy Spirit to do the teaching.

The book of James in my Bible is filled with notes I've written in the margin. In the column next to James chapter 1, I have listed the most trying times of my life over the past twenty-five years. I've noted my trials and the dates they occurred next to this chapter so I'll always remember the mighty works of God in each painful event. Just the fact that each of those trials are now over and that God brought me through each one is reason enough to be thankful. But I'm also thankful because each trial gifted me with some type of revelation—revealing parts of God or myself that were previously hidden to me. I can see how God developed my character and taught me to lean only on him in the face of each difficulty. I can also look at my list of trials and be confident that just as God brought me through each one of those, he will surely be faithful to me in the next trial, so I no longer fear what tomorrow holds—for that I'm truly thankful.

Trouble, indeed, knocks on every man's door. And when it does, we can turn to James chapter 1 for a glimpse into why we must endure it and also find instructions on how to respond to it. Let's see what

James, under the direction of the Holy Spirit, says about the trials we encounter.

> My brethren, count it all joy when you fall into various trials, knowing that the testing of your faith produces patience. But let patience have its perfect work, that you may be perfect and complete lacking nothing.
>
> James 1:2–4

The first thing we notice is that James is speaking to his "brethren," so we know that what follows is a word specifically written to followers of Christ. Let's focus on the phrase "when you fall into various trials." The word *fall* in the Greek is *peripipto. Strong's Exhaustive Concordance of the Bible* defines *peripipto* as: "to fall into something that is all around."

I'm reminded of a game our young married church group played outdoors one fall evening. The men were blindfolded and lined up ten yards opposite from their wives. In the grass between the men and women were several large, foaming piles of shaving cream. The goal of the game was for the wife to verbally guide her blindfolded husband through the maze of piles, without him stepping into the shaving cream. Not one husband made it across to his wife without falling into a pile of shaving cream. The piles could not be avoided because they were all around, just like the trials in our lives—they simply cannot be avoided.

Since the day that forbidden fruit was tasted in the garden, we all live in a fallen world. The world, the flesh, and the devil surround us. With every step we take, there is an opportunity to fall—because we're surrounded! Sometimes we see it coming; sometimes we're knocked off our feet before we know what hit us; sometimes it's our own negligence that makes us fall. But sooner or later, we all fall down. Now, let's look at what we fall into.

> My brethren, count it all joy when you fall into various trials.
>
> James 1:2

The Greek word translated above as *trials* is translated below as *temptations.*

> Let no one say when he is tempted, "I am tempted by God;" for God cannot be tempted by evil, nor does He Himself tempt anyone. But each one is tempted when he is drawn away by his own desires and enticed.
>
> James 1:13–14

The NIV Study Bible has a commentary on James 1:2 and James 1: 13–14 that says:

> In vv.2–3 the emphasis is on difficulties that come from outside; in vv.13–15 it is on inner moral trials such as temptation to sin.

So we need to understand that there is a big difference between a trial and a temptation. We'll all fall into trials because we live in a fallen world and they surround us. A trial might be persecution in the form of ridicule, rejection, or even physical torture. A trial could also be that your home is in the path of a tornado and you lose a lifetime of possessions. A trial could be the strain and heartache of caring for your aging parent suffering the devastating effects of dementia. Trials are all around us—and so are temptations.

We all are tempted. We all have areas of weakness that we must overcome, but they are unique to each person. You could put a case of beer and a pack of cigarettes on my kitchen counter, and I will never be tempted to imbibe in either—they don't appeal to me. But a bag of dark chocolate candy and a juicy piece of gossip just might get my attention! As the verse in James 1:14 says, we all have our "own desires," and we must strive not to give in to them, or we will experience some degree of death as a result. An example might be a woman who hears a piece of gossip about a new acquaintance. She then repeats that gossip to someone else, and—as gossip always does—it gets back to the other person, who is angry that she's being talked about. Two women have an opportunity to make a lasting friendship. But when one chooses to gossip about the other, not only will there not be a friendship formed, but any relationship between the two is highly unlikely. Gossip will kill the relationship. Sin brings death in one form or another; that's why it's critical that we fight against temptations that appeal to our flesh.

When I think of temptation, I'm reminded of cartoons that depict a person with a choice to either do good or evil. The cartoon character struggles with the decision to listen to the haloed white angel on one shoulder encouraging him to do the right thing, while a pitchfork-holding red devil sits on the other shoulder, whispering words to entice a selfish or evil act. That picture is actually fairly accurate. As Christians, we have the Holy Spirit inside us, whispering to us and encouraging us to make godly choices. At the same time, our flesh wants to fulfill its own desires, and Satan tries to talk us into following our fleshly desires. So we're left with an inner struggle—a choice to do right or do wrong; a choice of life or of death.

It is vital to point out that God never tempts us to sin. *The Wycliffe Bible Commentary* states:

> 13 The word temptation (v.12) carries the idea of luring one into sin. James probably had in mind the Jewish doctrine of the Yetzer ha ra,' "evil impulse." Some Jews reasoned that since God created everything, he must have created the evil impulse. And since it is the evil impulse that tempts man to sin, ultimately God, who created it, is responsible for evil. James here refutes that idea. God cannot be tempted with evil, neither tempteth he any man. 14. Instead of blaming God for evil, man must take personal responsibility for his sins. It is his own lust by which he is drawn away and enticed.

So to recap the study process so far, remember that trials come to all of us and they are pressures on us from without. Temptations come to all of us as well, and they are pressures from within to entice us to sin. God will never tempt you in the hope that you will sin. So with that squared away, let's return to our original questions of why trials come and scout for reasons God allows trials in our lives.

SOME TRIALS COME BECAUSE GOD IS TESTING YOUR FAITH

Knowing that the testing of your faith produces patience...

James 1:3

The refining pot is for silver and the furnace for gold, But the Lord tests the hearts.

Proverbs 17:3

I'm a child of the 1960s—the Beatles, flower power, peace, hippies, and the Cold War. I wasn't exactly sure who the Communists were, but I knew I should be afraid of them. The threat of an attack from Russia was a common fear for even little blond-haired girls like me who rode bicycles with banana seats. Now, I don't know why the Emergency Broadcast System started, but I'll assume it had something to do with communicating in the event of an attack from our nation's enemies. Occasionally, while watching our black and white television, a long, loud *beep* would sound and interrupt my cartoons with the familiar pattern of the Emergency Broadcast System. I would freeze in fear—wondering if the Russians were coming—until I heard the announcer calmly say, "Do not panic. This is only a test."

When a trial suddenly interrupts your day, what is your first reaction? Are you frozen in fear? Well, let me repeat those familiar words for you to apply in your situation: *Do not panic. This is only a test.* Yes, God will most surely test your faith—just try not to panic when he does.

So why does God test our faith? According to James 1:3, one reason is to produce patience in us. We've all probably heard the well-meaning advice from a friend to "Never pray for patience!" They say this because Scripture plainly tells us that patience comes through testing of our faith—and it's the painful parts of our testing that we never enjoy. However, the results *are* worth the pain because we grow up in the Lord and come into a maturity we would never have without the testing.

Who better to consider than Job, the man whose life is remembered for the horrendous tragedy and grief he endured? We read in Job that it was God who first brought up Job's name in his conversation with Satan. God removed the hedge of protection he had around Job and allowed Satan to wreak havoc in Job's life, although God gave Satan clear boundaries on what he could and could not touch. In a single day, Job lost all ten of his children and most of his wealth. Shortly thereafter, he was struck with a dreadful and painful disease. Despite the tragedy, this good and blameless man became an even better man. God chose to test Job's faith and record it for us to study thousands of years later. Read Job's thoughts on his testing and the end result it brought.

> But He knows the way that I take; when He has tested me, I shall come forth as gold.
>
> Job 23:10

There's an old phrase seldom used these days called "testing your metal." When a craftsman tests steel or refines precious metals, he must do it with extreme heat. This process allows for the impurities in the metal to be removed, thereby making for a stronger and more trustworthy metal. When God allows a fiery trial with extreme heat to come into our lives, it "tests our metal." God already knows what we're made of, but we don't, and those around us don't, until the flames get hot enough to reveal the weaknesses in our nature. As the heat reaches a higher degree, impurities in us are burned away, leaving a metal that has been tried by fire. If God is "testing your metal" today, be thankful for the flames that will soon bring you to rich fulfillment. There is a purpose in this pain.

> For You, O God, have proved us; You have refined us as silver is refined. You brought us into the net, You laid affliction on our backs. You have caused men to ride over our heads; we went through fire and through water; but You brought us out to rich fulfillment.
>
> Psalm 66:10–12

I've always admired the first United States astronauts. Those brave men truly had the "right stuff," but they were subjected to lengthy and difficult tests to prove it. The men in the program were tested on physical condition, their knowledge of equipment, and their abilities to perform under stress and maintain alertness. They were going to be launched into outer space, and there would be no turning back once the spaceship lifted off. The purpose of the tests was to prepare these pilots, not to hurt them, so they could confidently face the unknown in outer space. Simply put, the testing and training was for the pilot's own good. Think of the confidence these men had when they finally strapped themselves into the space rockets for takeoff. They had been tested, and they had discovered courage and strength inside themselves that may have never surfaced without the tests. If these brave men in the early space programs did not endure such severe testing, they may have faced the unknown with great dread and anxiety. Instead, they knew they had the "right stuff," and they displayed confidence because of their training. Without that rigorous testing and training, it's doubtful they could have accomplished their mission to explore the final frontier of space.

Do you suppose they were thankful for their training? I'll bet they were. Shouldn't we also be thankful for our spiritual training missions and testing? God is testing and training us to make us better and more capable to accomplish the missions he has for us.

If you still aren't convinced that a trial is good for you, let's look into the parable of the Pearl of Great Price. A parable is an earthly story with a heavenly meaning. As Jesus was teaching about the kingdom of heaven, he told this short story of a man who sold everything he owned so he could buy the most valuable pearl.

> Again, the kingdom of heaven is like a merchant seeking beautiful pearls, who, when he had found one pearl of great price, went and sold all that he had and bought it.
>
> Matthew 13:45–46

Most of my church life, I've been taught that Jesus is the pearl of great price, and of course in one sense, he is. But many Bible scholars teach that this parable is actually a reference to the church for the following reasons. Pearls come from oysters, which are not a kosher food. The church is predominantly made up of Gentiles, which were considered unclean—not kosher—in Jewish law. Jesus sold all that he had—himself—to purchase the church. Of all the jewels, the pearl is the only one that comes from a living thing as opposed to being found in the earth. Now, here's the connection to trials: a pearl is formed by an irritation. The more irritation, the more it grows! Like the pearl, the church—comprised of individuals—must endure irritations to grow. Just as a pearl isn't formed overnight, neither will we come into beauty and value quickly, but only after years of irritating trials. A mature pearl must be removed from its birthplace to see its true beauty, which comes only when it reflects light. When Jesus removes us from our birthplace, and we reside in heaven with him, we will completely reflect the light of Christ and reveal our true beauty as his bride. It is the plan of God to expose the beautiful and valuable pearl his grace has made us to be. He had a purpose for allowing every irritation in our lives—to create a pearl of great price. Oh, be thankful for the irritations that form you into a precious jewel and cause you to reflect his Holy light.

The Gospel of John clearly records evidence of God testing our faith. Jesus was gaining popularity for the many miracles he had performed, and this caused a curious multitude of people to follow him. Jesus and his disciples sat on a mountain near the Sea of Galilee and looked over this large crowd. The nearest town was Bethsaida, the disciple Philip's hometown, and it was too far away and too late an hour to get food to feed such a crowd.

> Then Jesus lifted up His eyes, and seeing a great multitude coming toward Him, He said to Philip, "Where shall we buy bread, that these may eat?" But this He said to test him, for He Himself knew what He would do.
>
> John 6:5–6

The Greek word translated *test* above is the word *peiradzo*. According to Rick Renner's *Sparkling Gems from the Greek*, *peiradzo* means "to test in order to expose the truth about the quality of a substance." In a spiritual situation, the purpose of the test is not to do damage or to humiliate or embarrass someone, but to make the person better. In this gospel story, Philip considered natural means to feed the multitude, concluding that the crowd was so large they didn't have enough money to buy food for them all.

The crowd was eventually counted, and the men alone numbered five thousand. If we factor in women and children who were surely also in the crowd, there could have been upwards of ten thousand hungry tummies in that crowd. For a moment, let's focus on the impossible task of feeding a crowd of *just* five thousand. Even today—with our modern microwave appliances and cell phone communications—feeding five thousand people on a moment's notice is impossible. Even with a few hours' notice, it's still not likely to happen, especially when an unprepared and unsuspecting group of twelve men is expected to pay for it! Philip's desperate search for food by natural means revealed his lack of faith. He should have immediately seen the situation for what it was, impossible in the natural. Only God could handle the situation. This faith test exposed a weakness in Philip's faith—he tried to fix the problem with his own natural means.

The story continues with Jesus miraculously feeding the multitude with only five loaves of bread and two small fish. The crowd feasted until they were full, and then twelve baskets of leftovers were gathered. After this, Philip—and the other disciples—realized they had a long way to go in the faith department. Without that faith test, they wouldn't recognize their weakness in looking to the natural before the spiritual.

Has Jesus tested your faith already and exposed a weak area in your life? I've had more of these tests and exposures than I care to admit. Remember, the tests do not come to reveal our weaknesses to God, for he knows our every weakness already. But the tests come so that our blinded—and often prideful—eyes can see ourselves more clearly. This clarity of vision will expose the truth about our quality, all for our own good and hopeful improvement. Be thankful when God exposes a weakness in your faith; it's only then that you can let him perfect that area in you.

———————◆———————

School was a perfect fit for me. I liked rules and structure, and I had a heart to please and a strong desire to succeed. My name was always on the honor roll. Knowing this about me, you may find it hard to believe that the last day of elementary school each year was pure torture for me. That was the day my report card was passed out to reveal whether or not I was promoted to the next grade or required to repeat the same grade. I remember my heart pounding and my little palms sweating with nervous anxiety until I looked at my report card and saw whether or not I was promoted to the next grade. Obviously, as an A+ student, I was always promoted, despite my worst fears and self-doubt.

When we compare school life to our spiritual lives, there is a strong similarity. In school, students in each grade are required to learn certain subjects and then take tests to prove that they have sufficiently learned those subjects. At the end of the year, the passing students are then promoted to the next grade. Then the process begins all over again in the next grade. Each new level requires more of the students' time and energy as they learn and develop new skills. But the ultimate goal at each level is to pass and be promoted. We understand this process in the educational system; why is it so hard for us to grasp the same concept in the spiritual system? God expects us to learn and grow—and he will test us before he promotes us.

An unknown young man who studied the Law of God wrote Psalm 119. Notice how he lists the progression of being taught, going through the test of affliction, realizing the benefit of the whole process, and then most of all, understanding the goodness of God. This young man was taught, tested, and promoted, all for his own good.

You have dealt well with Your servant, O Lord, according to Your word. Teach me good judgment and knowledge, for I believe Your commandments. Before I was afflicted I went astray, but now I keep Your word. You are good, and do good; teach me Your statutes. The proud have forged a lie against me, but I will keep Your precepts with my whole heart. Their heart is as fat as grease, but I delight in Your law. It is good for me that I have been afflicted, that I may learn Your statutes. The law of Your mouth is better to me than thousands of shekels of gold and silver.

Psalm 119:65–72

SOME TRIALS COME BECAUSE OF YOUR OWN POOR CHOICES

Do not be deceived, God is not mocked; for whatever a man sows, that he will also reap.

Galatians 6:7

My dear friend and pastor for many years was a man named Ed McGavock. He had a genuine love for people that I've seldom seen exhibited in any other man. Although he had this great love for his congregation, he didn't hesitate to preach the gospel straight up— even if the message painfully stepped all over our toes. One Sunday he was preaching on the biblical principal of reaping what you sow. With a toothy grin and sparkling eyes, he leaned toward the congregation and said, "Some of you may be praying for crop failure!"

Most of us probably have pleaded with God for crop failure where we've sown seeds of sin. God has set principles in motion on this earth, and reaping/sowing is one of the most obvious. The world has a saying for this same principle: "What goes around comes around!" When you plant okra, you won't be surprised when okra sprouts up. So when you do wrong by your brother, don't be surprised when you are done wrong in return. The good news is that this principal works just the same for good. When you do right by others, right will be done for you.

So what about your mistakes? Are you doomed and depressed

because of the seeds you've sown? Don't fret, sweet child of God, and be thankful because God is also merciful, promising to restore what the locust has eaten. However, most of the time when God hears you pray for "crop failure," he'll likely answer with the grace to endure your harvest, and that grace will be most sufficient.

In my early twenties, I worked as a bank teller. When the holidays rolled around, so did the annual employee Christmas party, and it was booked at a classy restaurant overlooking the lake. My husband and I—with a toddler at home and Christmas bearing down upon us—were barely making our financial ends meet. But I really, really wanted a new dress to wear to this ritzy party. I only had one credit card, and it was to an expensive department store. With marked determination, I set out to find the perfect party dress. Once inside the expensive department store, I found *the* dress. It was black and white taffeta with a ruffled collar, a cute little bowtie at the neckline, and a big, black bow that perfectly fit the small of my back. In 1983, that style of dress was quite fashionable! I handed my charge card to the nice lady at the register, and in moments I walked out of that store with *the* dress—and $200 of debt. Looking back on that event, I'd like to blame it on a hormone imbalance, some weird psychotic episode, or being deprived as a child…but I cannot. I did a foolish thing—spending that kind of money for a dress to impress people I worked with—and I had no one to blame but myself for sowing seeds of selfishness and pride. The seeds were sown, and the harvest would come quickly and last a long, long time.

The night of the party arrived, and it was so fun to dress up for our first really grown-up party. Buddy looked so handsome in his gray pinstripe suit, and I imagined all the attention and compliments my dress would surely draw. We were seated at a table in the dark restaurant among my coworkers and their spouses. Like most office Christmas parties, the atmosphere early on was polite and quiet, but once the alcohol was served, people became more—shall we say—at ease. Buddy and I, as nondrinkers, felt uncomfortable and out of place. We didn't want to be rude by leaving early, so we waited until our steaks were served and we began to eat. While we were enjoying our delicious meal in that small, dark, crowded dining room, one of the waitresses carrying a tray of drinks past our table was bumped. A drink from her tray fell, and would you like to guess where that alcoholic beverage landed? All down the side and back of my new $200 taffeta dress—which, by the way, not one person had complimented me on! It was ruined as far as I was concerned because I couldn't afford to pay a dry cleaner to clean it.

For two years, I paid the minimum payment of ten dollars a month on that credit card until that dress was finally paid off. What was I thinkin'—that Santa Claus would leave the money for that dress in my stocking? What a poor, poor choice on my part. Since that day, I don't think I've paid more than fifty dollars for any dress I've purchased for myself. Lesson learned: you will reap what you sow, and debts must be paid, even if the charged item has lost its worth and you think you've lost your mind.

SOME TRIALS COME BECAUSE OF SOMEBODY ELSE'S POOR CHOICES

But may the God of all grace, who called us, to His eternal glory by Christ Jesus, after you have suffered a while, perfect, establish, strengthen, and settle you.

1 Peter 5:10

Second Samuel 21 tells a sad story about a loving mother named Rizpah. She was King Saul's concubine, and she bore him two sons. The Bible doesn't specifically record any wrongdoings by Rizpah or her sons. Saul, however, did sin before the Lord.

The Gibeonites had been in covenant with the Israelites since the days of Joshua (see Joshua 9). This covenant basically made the Gibeonites slaves but gave them protection among the children of Israel. Saul broke this covenant—which was sworn before the Lord—when he zealously tried to annihilate the Gibeonites. Years later, Saul was dead and David was king over all Israel and Judah. A three-year famine came on the land because of Saul's sin against the Gibeonites. When David asked the Gibeonites what could be done to atone for Saul's bloodthirsty action, the Gibeonites asked for seven of Saul's descendants—they planned to hang them. Rizpah's two sons, along with five of their half-brothers, were handed over to foreigners to be hanged—all because of their father's sin.

On a lonely hill outside of town, seven innocent young men were hung. Seven brothers killed to pay for their father's sin. Seven bodies left to dangle and decay in the elements without a proper burial. Seven executed sons, two grieving mothers—and only one of them chose to consider the dignity of her sons over her own well-being. Rizpah stayed at the gruesome scene, clothed in sackcloth and ashes. Every day—all day long—she fought to keep the birds from pecking at her boys' bodies. Every night—all night long—she struggled to stay awake so she could keep the wild animals from trying to consume the flesh she had given birth to. This pitiful ritual didn't last for a day or two—it didn't last for a week or two—but Rizpah faithfully defended her sons' remains for five long, weary months.

I cannot begin to imagine the unbearable heartache this woman experienced. The death of your child—at any age—is tragic, but to see your innocent sons brutally murdered and not even get a proper burial for them is more than any mother should bear. To make matters worse, Rizpah had been a concubine. She had no status or respect in society. She was the concubine of a dead king who had been the enemy of the current king; whom did she have to comfort her? Did people suppose she didn't have any feelings, that she loved her sons less than they loved theirs? She walked a grief-laden road—alone—because of someone else's sin.

Even in this most tragic story, we see the merciful hand of God. King David heard of Rizpah's plight and out of compassion for her, ordered a proper and honorable burial for the victims. God then honored this mother when he established a written record of Rizpah's love and commitment to her children. Rizpah's heart was put through this tragic trial through no fault of her own. Someone else made a poor choice, and she and her sons suffered the consequences.

We can also observe cases where the poor choices of a country's leader—or leaders—will bring God's judgment on the entire nation. That's one reason I believe Christians ought to prayerfully consider candidates before they step in the voting booth. As Christians, we are accountable to God for our actions, and I believe that includes the leaders we vote into office. The decisions our leaders make in office won't just affect our tax dollars and the condition of the roads we drive on. When leaders legislate ungodly laws in our society—as they have already done—God notices, and he does judge sin. The poor choices of our leaders can bring trial to us all. This happened when King David sinned against God when he counted the people. In 2 Samuel 24, David ordered a census. This chapter doesn't explain exactly why this particular census was a sin. Perhaps it had something to do with David trusting in his own military might or being puffed up about his mighty kingdom. But whatever the reason, it was a sin—and David knew it. David later repented; and God, who is merciful, is also just, and he judged David's sin. Through the Prophet Gad, God allowed David to choose his judgment. David could choose either seven years of famine, three months of running from his enemies, or a three-day plague across the land. David, with a repentant heart, made a choice that proved he completely trusted his merciful God.

> And David said to Gad, "I am in great distress. Please let us fall into the hand of the Lord, for His mercies are great; but do not let me fall into the hand of man." So the Lord sent a plague upon Israel from the morning till the appointed time. From Dan to Beersheba seventy thousand men of the people died. And when the angel stretched out His hand over Jerusalem to destroy it, the Lord relented from the destruction, and said to the angel who was destroying the people, "It is enough; now restrain Your hand."
>
> 2 Samuel 24:14–16

This passage might be a tough one for you to swallow. It is not a case where God removes a hedge of protection and allows Satan to come in and destroy. It is God himself judging sin by the hand of the angel of the Lord. Notice the capitalization of "Your" in the verse above. This indicates that the translator believes the angel is divine. You may need to chew on this one a little while. I love the fact that David preferred what *God* would do to him rather than what *man* would do to him. David knew he was not appointed to God's wrath—but loving discipline instead. Painful, yes; but love was God's motive. His judgments are always true and meant to draw us back to him.

The difficult part of this story is to try explaining why seventy thousand innocent men died in a plaque because of David's sin. I cannot explain it or understand it, but it does not change my belief in the loving nature of God Almighty. But like Rizpah's situation, someone else's sin can trickle down and bring pain to those around them. We just have to trust God and still keep a thankful heart as we remind ourselves that God is always merciful, loving, and just—even when we cannot explain the painful things he allows in our lives.

Perhaps you're walking a hard and rocky road because of someone else's sin. Dear one, your good God can use that rocky road to perfect, establish, strengthen, and settle you—after you've suffered.

SOME TRIALS COME BECAUSE YOU'RE IN REBELLION

For the time has come for judgment to begin at the house of God.

1 Peter 4:17

Achan had sticky fingers, and he thought his stolen items were safely hidden away buried in the dirt beneath his tent, but sin can never be hidden from the Lord. Joshua 6 and 7 tell of the great fall of the walls of Jericho and the rebellion of a man named Achan. You know how the old song goes: "Joshua fit de battle of Jericho ... and de walls came a tumblin' down." It was a spectacular display of the awesome power of God as he gave his people their first victory in claiming the land God had promised them. Following God's instructions, Joshua led the children of Israel as they marched around the city seven times in a single day, and when the priests blew their trumpets in one long blast, all the people shouted and the mighty walls of Jericho fell down flat.

God had given specific instructions for the battle against Jericho. No one in the city but Rahab and her family were to be spared. No one was to keep for himself any silver or gold—that was all for the Lord's treasury only. One of the Israelites was a man named Achan, whose greed was strong. In disobedience to God's command not to keep any of the spoils of this war, Achan secretly stole—and hid in his tent—exactly what God said not to. Because of Achan's rebellion, the Bible says the anger of the Lord burned against the children of Israel.

After the Jericho victory, Joshua led the confident Israelites into battle against the city of Ai. It should have been an easy fight, but instead the Israelites were chased back to camp in defeat. Joshua cried out to God for an explanation, and that's when God revealed that there was sin in the camp! Through a process of elimination orchestrated by God, Achan was brought forth as the perpetrator, and he confessed to taking the forbidden valuables. Achan, along with his whole family and his livestock, were killed, and then their remains and all their possessions were burned.

You may be ready to put this book down, thinking I'm a doom-and-gloom writer who sees God anxiously waiting for his people to mess up so he can hurt them. That is not at all the point of this book, so please bear with me while I continue. I believe a loving heavenly Father wants to stop sin from spreading through the camp. The camp could be our own family, our workplace, or even our church. When we sin, it affects those around us—whether we mean for it to or not. God will expose and judge our sin for the sake of us all. Again, it's the goodness of God that exposes the sin and brings judgment, protecting us all from the contagious nature of sin.

God could not overlook Achan's rebellion. Will God overlook our rebellion today? I don't think so. Our heavenly Father will discipline us for our own good because he loves us and he wants to have fellowship with us.

Those whom I love I rebuke and discipline. So be earnest, and repent. Here I am! I stand at the door and knock. If anyone hears my voice and opens the door, I will come in and eat with him, and he with me.

Revelation 3:19 (NIV)

———◆———

If you and I compared notes from our childhood Sunday school experiences, I'll bet we could find many similarities. Small, brown metal folding chairs lined up against a concrete block wall painted a bright color of teal; a prim and proper gray-haired lady taught the Word of God to a room full of squirming boys and girls; a little cardboard church with a slit on the top just wide enough to put offering coins in; an old, upright, out-of-tune piano in the corner; and on the wall hung a colorful painting of Jesus knocking on a cottage door. Sound familiar?

For most of my life, I believed that picture represented Jesus knocking on the heart's door of the lost soul. But the verse comes from a letter written to a church. Jesus is speaking to saved people who were living lukewarm lives of sin and were not in close fellowship with Jesus. When our sin puts a divider between us and our Savior, he will discipline us because he wants us to be intimately close to him. What a loving Savior he is, and what fools we are to ignore his knocking and resist his discipline.

Whoever loves instruction loves knowledge, but he who hates reproof is stupid.

Proverbs 12:1

My momma didn't raise no fool, did yours? If we hate to be corrected, the New King James Version Bible says we are *stupid*. I think the verse above may step on all our toes, as I know no one who really *loves* correction. Will we ever learn that instruction and correction are for our own good? It's just like when parents discipline their own children. It's always for the children's own good—to teach and train them, not punish them. And the motive behind the discipline given them is a deep love for them. But seldom do children see that a swat on their behind for defiant disobedience is in their best interest. God loves us more than any parent is capable of loving his or her own children—and he won't hesitate to swat us when we need it. The point is, God loves us and he will discipline us to bring us back to him or to purge out of us qualities that are not Christlike.

I love the story of Elijah as told in 1 Kings 17. The people were living in outright rebellion to the Lord, as they worshiped the idol Baal. Elijah prophesied there would be no rain—or even dew—in Israel until he said so. Not a drop of water fell from the sky for three long, hot, dry, hungry, and thirsty years.

Here in Oklahoma, during the years 2005 and 2006, we suffered through severe drought, and I can tell you that it certainly took a toll on our entire state. Farmers had their crops fail. Ranchers had to sell their cattle out of state because there wasn't enough water for them to drink in the summer and not enough hay for them to eat in the winter. Dry conditions and high winds caused the tiniest sparks to start blazing wildfires that wrought havoc in multiple counties—including my own. During that time, we had at least some intermittent rain in small amounts, but in Elijah's day, Israel received no rain or dew for all three years. This lack of water led to severe famine in Israel.

The story continues in 1 Kings 18 when Elijah and wicked King Ahab meet face-to-face. Ahab was king of Israel and was married to the infamous Jezebel, who had just slaughtered all but one hundred prophets of God. Her controlling, manipulating influence over King Ahab led to the worship of Baal throughout Israel. Elijah told Ahab to bring all of Israel to Mount Carmel, along with the four hundred fifty prophets of Baal and the four hundred prophets of Asherah— another idol that the people worshiped. At Mount Carmel, Elijah challenged the prophets of Baal to a fire-making contest between Baal and the Lord God—whichever god sent fire to consume the sacrificial offering would determine the real God. Elijah prayed, and the Lord God sent fire to consume the sacrifice as well as the wood, the stones, the dust, and even the water Elijah drenched it all with!

Pay close attention to the prayer Elijah prayed just before he called down fire from heaven.

> Hear me, O Lord, hear me, that this people may know that You are the Lord God, and that You have turned their hearts back to You again.
>
> 1 Kings 18:37

The question is: without the drought or the fire challenge, would the people have come to their senses and returned to God on their own? I think it's doubtful. Elijah understood that it was God who was turning the hearts of his people back to him—again. Once the people came back to the Lord, he was merciful and sent rain upon their land. So was the drought something to be thankful for? Most definitely! Their rebellion was followed by a discipline trial—called drought—and that ultimately brought the people back to God.

Some may argue that God only disciplined his people in the Old Testament, but we Christians today are under grace. Praise God that we are living in the days of grace. But let's examine Hebrews 12 and see if God is finished with discipline.

> Looking unto Jesus, the author and finisher of our faith …
>
> Hebrews 12:2

Jesus is described in this verse as being the "author and finisher of our faith." Any spiritual maturity we achieve is because of his work in us; we could never accomplish anything spiritually all by ourselves. Since Jesus is the finisher of our faith, he will have to do whatever it takes to progress us along in our spiritual journey. Our cooperation with him affects the outcome, but if we belong to him, in the end, Jesus will finish his work in us. Be assured that Jesus takes his job as finisher of our faith very seriously. Hebrews 12 continues with an emphasis on the discipline of God in the life of Christians.

My son, do not despise the chastening of the Lord, nor be discouraged when you are rebuked by Him; for whom the Lord loves He chastens, and scourges every son whom He receives. If you endure chastening, God deals with you as with sons; for what son is there whom a father does not chasten? But if you are without chastening, of which all have become partakers, then you are illegitimate and not sons. Furthermore, we have had human fathers who corrected us, and we paid them respect. Shall we not much more readily be in subjection to the Father of spirits and live? For they indeed for a few days chastened us as seemed best to them, but He for our profit, that we may be partakers of His holiness. Now no chastening seems to be joyful for the present, but grievous; nevertheless, afterward it yields the peaceable fruit of righteousness to those who have been trained by it.

Hebrews 12:5–11

This passage tells us that the Lord will chastise us because he loves us and he wants us to be trained by that chastisement, which results in our righteousness, even though we may scream and cry through the whole process. *Chastise* isn't a common word in our daily language, so we need to discover its true meaning. Rick Renner comments in *Sparkling Gems from the Greek* that chastening in Hebrews 12:11 means "disciplinary attitudes and actions that lead to one's betterment in life or to one's education."

So we can conclude that when the Lord sees us in outright rebellion, or maybe just starting to head in the wrong direction, as the finisher of our faith, he takes the responsibility to discipline us for our own betterment in life or our education. Of course, the trick to all this for you and me is paying attention to the discipline and learning from it.

My sister Sissy is just eleven months younger than I am. We're the first two of four girls—all born between 1960 and 1964. Even though Momma had her hands full with four stair-stepped little girls, there really wasn't a lot of drama in our house. We fought like sisters do—name calling, hair pulling, tattling, and the like—but for the most part, we had a healthy fear of Momma, and she kept us in line through the day. That is, except for Sissy, the rebel among us, whose defiant facial expressions alone exasperated our patient momma. Whenever Momma tried to discipline Sissy, the fight was on! Sissy insisted on talking back and having the last word when Momma got on to her.

Momma's response to talking back was the same as all the other mommas in the 1960s: she washed her kids' mouths out with soap! Now, I've never tasted a bar of soap, but as I watched Sissy's first experience at the sink with it, I decided that was not for me. I learned that talking back to Momma had a consequence I didn't want to face. Sissy, on the other hand, wasn't as quick to catch on. More than once she was forced to taste the bitter bar of Ivory soap while Momma washed her mouth out with it. Even after the mouth washing, with tears in her squinted eyes and soapy bubbles coming out of her mouth, she would stand up, look Momma straight in the eye, and talk back again! I would watch, horrified, and think, *Why doesn't she just shut up? Doesn't she understand she's just making it worse?* Then round two would begin.

Sissy's stubborn rebellion refused to submit to authority, and this cycle played out in our house for years. Momma held her ground, and Sissy is all the better for it today. It's easy for her to joke about it now, but man, oh man; she could have saved herself a lot of grievous pain if she'd just learned the lesson the first time!

Today I see adult Christians doing the same thing my baby sister did as a child—rebelling and not learning the lesson. It's plain to see that their trial is the discipline of God for their own good, yet their stubborn rebellion continues and they remain in trouble. These are the people who have a slight variation of the same trial over and over and over—because they won't learn! If that describes you, please yield your heart to the one who has your best interest in his own heart. The quicker you learn, the quicker the trial can end.

Our daughter, Sarah Jane, whom we call Janie, was a curious and independent child. Unlike her brother, who always stayed obediently by Daddy and Momma, Janie would see something of interest to her and run right to it. One day when Janie was four, our family was in a sixty-story building for a doctor appointment. While Buddy and I asked a receptionist for directions in this huge building, Janie bolted for the shiny, gold elevator doors. As I ran after her, my mind raced in those few seconds, wondering how we would find her if I couldn't get to the elevator doors before they closed. I was terrified as I imagined six elevators servicing a sixty-story building and the multitude of possibilities of where our pig-tailed little girl might end up and who might take advantage of her. By the grace of God, I arrived at the elevator door just as it closed, and I was able to pry it open. There she stood, wide-eyed, at the back of the elevator, wondering if she was going to get a spanking—and she did, right after I held her close for one very long, thankful moment.

Shortly after the elevator episode we went on vacation to Six Flags over Texas. With Janie's history of intense curiosity and boldness, we decided she should wear one of those child leashes—for her own safety. It was two Velcro wrist bracelets attached by a line that resembled a telephone cord. She was smart enough to know how to undo Velcro, so we had to dress her in a pair of overall shorts and attach the leash to the back of them. The leash provided us peace of mind and gave Janie a cord's length of freedom to move around.

While strolling through Six Flags, we entered an area where a puppet show was in progress. We stopped and stood in the back of the crowd so our kids could watch. The puppeteer noticed us, pointed us out to the seated crowd and said, "Hey, look! There's a lady with a kid on a leash! Ma'am, don't you know this is an amusement park, not an abusement park!" I blushed in embarrassment as the crowd laughed, but I still kept my Janie on that leash—for her own good. As her momma, I knew better than the puppeteer or the crowd what was in my daughter's heart. I knew how her curiosity tempted her to wander off alone even in strange places. She had to have a boundary for her own protection until she learned what was safe and what was not. It was my tremendous love for her that kept her in the confinement of a leash.

Doesn't your heavenly Father know your heart and your temptations better than even you do? He may have to keep you in an uncomfortable or confined place until you learn what is safe for you and what is dangerous for you. In other words, until you come into more maturity, you may be kept uncomfortable because of your heavenly Father's great love for you. You may accuse God of being mean to you. That's not his nature. Your trial could be a manifestation of his love and protection for you. When you mature in him, you'll clearly be able to see his loving, protecting hand.

> You answered them, O Lord our God; You were to them God-Who-Forgives, though You took vengeance on their deeds.
>
> Psalm 99:8

Understand that there is a big difference between being disciplined by God and having his wrath fall on you. God's love for us is the motive behind his discipline—and we need not fear his discipline. He disciplines us because of our deeds and our actions. But, as the verse above says, he is the God-Who-Forgives! Now, the wrath of God is entirely different. God's people receive his loving discipline, never his wrath. The wrath of God is reserved for those who reject Christ, as we see in Revelation 6—and those people should be afraid, very afraid. Be thankful when God disciplines you and learn the lesson quickly. And if you belong to Christ, also be thankful that he has spared you from his wrath.

> For God did not appoint us to wrath but to obtain salvation through our Lord Jesus Christ.
>
> 1 Thessalonians 5:9

> And said to the mountains and rocks, "Fall on us, and hide us from the face of Him who sits on the throne and from the wrath of the Lamb! For the great day of His wrath has come, and who is able to stand?"
>
> Revelation 6:16–17

SOME TRIALS COME BECAUSE YOU LIVE IN A FALLEN WORLD

These things I have spoken to you, that in Me you may have peace.
In the world you will have tribulation; but be of good cheer, I have
overcome the world.

John 16:33

When my son, Andy, was a little boy, he used to ask me, "Momma, what if Adam never sinned? Things would be a lot better, wouldn't they?"

"They would be a whole lot better, honey!" I replied. "But even if Adam hadn't sinned, the next ol' boy would have, and we'd be in the same boat we're in today."

Yes, we live in a fallen, cursed world. Aggravation, workin' for a livin,' sorrow, and temptation all come with it. Somewhere a flu virus is waiting for you on the handle of a shopping cart, dogs dig in flowerbeds, hailstorms ruin roofs, some people are mean, and someone you love will die. If you live in this world, you'll have sorrow in it, and there's no avoiding all of it. However, I do believe we can avoid *some* of it. But we cannot avoid *all* sorrow because we do live in a fallen world. The good news is that sorrow can be a bridge to a better side of you if you allow God to do a work in you. It's up to you whether you let trials and sorrows make you wiser and stronger or weaker and more self-centered. The best person you can be is buried deep inside you, waiting to emerge peacefully, after it is purged in the fires of sorrow.

No temptation has overtaken you except such as is common to man; but God is faithful, who will not allow you to be tempted beyond what you are able, but with the temptation will also make the way of escape, that you may be able to bear it.

1 Corinthians 10:13

Another problem with living in a fallen world is the unavoidable temptation to sin. We're all in this temptation boat together, and there is just no way around it. It is common to man. We all have our own particular weaknesses, and you can count on being tempted wherever your flesh is weak. Your weakness might be a quick temper, a lustful eye, or not telling the truth.

Did you give in to your temptation and now you are paying the price for it? You don't have to go down that path again. Look again at the verse above. God wants you to be an overcomer, and he is faithful not to allow you to be tempted to the point you just can't say no to that temptation. He offers you a plan of escape and a way you can bear it. Don't beat yourself up because you were tempted—no one can keep the temptations from coming. But the next time temptation rears its ugly head, you can run to your Daddy God, knowing that he provides a way of escape.

SOME TRIALS COME TO MAKE YOU STRONGER

Who is the man that fears the Lord? Him shall He teach in the way He chooses.

Psalm 25:12

Proverbs 6 tells us to consider the ant and her hardworking ways. Well, in this section of the book, may I suggest that you consider the weightlifter? Wouldn't you like to have nicely toned and chiseled muscles and a low percentage of body fat? I certainly would, but I'm not sure I'm committed to do everything that's required to look that way! People with buff bodies weren't born that way. The bodybuilder has invested time and energy to achieve a nice-looking body, sacrificing a junk-food diet and spending many disciplined hours on exercise and strength training.

What does bodybuilding have to do with trials? When we lift weights, we actually tear the muscle. That sounds bad, but it's really good. As the torn muscle rebuilds, it comes back stronger than it was before the tear. So when you face a test or a trial, you may feel torn—and boy, does it hurt for a while—but not to worry, you'll come back stronger for it!

I loved my second grade teacher. She was probably not all that old when she taught my class, but to my seven-year-old eyes, she was ancient. I watched her very closely as she wrote our lessons on the big blackboard that covered the entire wall behind her desk. She wrote with perfect penmanship, and I was determined to learn and do well on my lessons. But those weren't the reasons I watched her so intently. Nope, instead I was mesmerized at how the flab on her arm would flop and wave back and forth each time she stroked the chalk across that board.

While getting ready for church many moons later, I glanced in the bathroom mirror and caught a glimpse of my own bare arm as I held a curling iron in my hair high above my head. To my utter shock and dismay, I saw my own flabby arm making the same flopping motion that I had watched while sitting in my second grade desk. This was not a happy discovery, as I saw what years of neglect had accomplished on my triceps muscle.

The painful truth is this: the triceps muscle—that lies somewhere under all my fat and flab—is still there. I know I was born with it, but no one knows it's there because they can't see it. However, I've recently started to work out on a Bow-flex machine—a machine my husband insisted he needed. Funny, he doesn't use it, but I do. I hate working my triceps muscle; it's very weak, and it doesn't take long for it to burn when I work it. But I am starting to see some progress. I'm actually working it out! My hope is that before I die of old age, my triceps muscle will be visible once again—if it ever was in the first place. But if I fail to *work them out*, one day some little kid is going to be mesmerized at the way my arm flips and flops.

Therefore, my beloved, as you have always obeyed, not as in my presence only, but now much more in my absence, work out your own salvation with fear and trembling; for it is God who works in you both to will and to do for His good pleasure.

Philippians 2:12–13

I don't believe this passage means we must earn our salvation or work hard to keep it. Rather, I believe it's speaking to believers and encouraging them to let their inner salvation show outwardly for all to see.

Do you see the similarities between weightlifting and spiritual conditioning? We all start out as babes in Christ, and our spirituality isn't very evident. When a trial enters our lives, we will feel torn and broken down. But we can continue working out our salvation by obeying the Lord and following him. Oh, it will be painful—and it may take a while—but the adversity can be the impetus that reveals the Christ that dwells in us. By God's grace we can successfully work out our salvation, and eventually be proud to show what God has done in our lives.

You have tested my heart.

Psalm 17:3

Just as the weightlifter gradually adds more weight to gain more strength, be prepared for God to allow heavier burdens and testing on you. He may have a mission for you that requires great strength. Just like the body builder doesn't bulk up overnight, neither does the new babe in Christ. Your spiritual muscles will be torn—a little at a time—so God can rebuild them even stronger. Never forget that he always has your best interest in mind.

For He has torn, but He will heal us; He has stricken, but He will bind us up.

Hosea 6:1

Simon Peter is an example of this tearing down and rebuilding stronger. Mark 14 records how the night before Jesus was crucified, he told his disciples that they would be made to stumble because of him. Peter spoke up and made his famous proclamation that even if everyone else stumbled he would not! That's when Jesus told Peter that before the rooster crowed that very night, Peter would have denied him three times. Upon hearing Jesus' prediction, Peter was all the more adamant in defending his faithfulness to Jesus, even exclaiming that he was willing to die with him. The Gospel of Luke records an additional part of this same conversation.

> And the Lord said, "Simon, Simon! Indeed, Satan has asked for you, that he may sift you as wheat. But I have prayed for you, that your faith should not fail; and when you have returned to Me, strengthen your brethren."
>
> Luke 22:31–32

Notice that Satan had to ask God's permission to sift Peter. I'm so thankful and I find it very comforting to know that Satan cannot touch us without God's permission. God is always in control to bring a greater good.

Satan wanted to sift Peter to tear him down, probably because he was the apparent leader of the disciples. *Sift* is a word associated with wheat. When wheat is sifted, it goes through a violent shaking that causes the dirt and debris to be separated from the good grain of the wheat. The good and bad are both exposed in the process of sifting, and the bad is sifted away from the good. Peter was sifted and his weakness was exposed when he denied even knowing Jesus. Satan meant to tear Peter down in the sifting; God's intent was to rebuild him stronger than ever once his weakness was sifted out of him.

Peter failed the ultimate test; he denied Christ. But that's not where his story ends. Peter did emerge from his denial of Christ to lead the disciples, strengthening them just as Jesus told him to do. Peter, a former failure, preached to a crowd on the Day of Pentecost and saw three thousand souls saved. Peter started off his journey with Jesus as a man with weak flesh. He was broken and rebuilt—stronger—by the grace of God. Today, you and I can read Peter's story and relate it to our own failures. We can be encouraged when we realize that God doesn't throw anyone away—no matter how weak they are—because he can rebuild us all stronger than ever.

It may seem disheartening to know that God would allow us

to endure something at the hand of Satan. Peter's example shows us that if God does allow us to be sifted, we can be thankful and assured of a few things. First, we have a great Intercessor, seated at the right hand of the Father—"but I have prayed for you that your faith should not fail." The second thing to remember is that God sees our outcome—"and when you have returned to me." He won't permit anything that doesn't justify the pain you'll endure. The third thing to know is that our sifting process can make us a blessing to someone else—"strengthen your brethren." Peter was in Jesus' inner circle of disciples and a leader among them. What an encouragement his testimony must have been to the other disciples—who also abandoned Jesus—and to any other Christian who may have also failed Jesus. All those who feel like failures can look to Peter and see that even if they've denied the Lord, Jesus is praying for them and there can always be restoration. The sifted soul, made stronger by the trial, can strengthen and encourage others. Be thankful for the test that makes you stronger.

SOME TRIALS COME FROM A LACK OF KNOWLEDGE

My people are destroyed for lack of knowledge.

Hosea 4:6

Our son, Andy, had just turned one year old when his Grandma Sarah gave him his first Fudgsicle. I had always been strict with his diet, allowing very little sugar, so this was a special occasion in my mom's kitchen when I nodded my permission for her to give it to him. Andy was still small enough to sit in his baby carrier, and we sat him on the kitchen table so everyone could watch him eat his first Fudgsicle.

Grandma put the frozen treat to his little mouth so he could have a taste. He loved it! He kicked his little feet in excitement and reached for it, insisting he hold it all by himself. The only problem was trying to show him how to hold the stick. He didn't understand, and every time we tried to put his hands on the stick, he screamed and cried, thinking we were trying to take away his treat. He didn't know to hold the frozen Fudgsicle by the stick, and instead he held it on its cold, cold sides. It didn't take long for his tiny fingers to feel freezing pain. Over and over, Andy would take a bite of the Fudgsicle and then let out a painful cry, but he refused to let go of it. I have to admit we were all laughing hysterically at him. There was just no helping him. He screamed if we took it away, and he screamed with the stinging pain of cold little fingers if he held it. After a few minutes of this, I finally had to take the Fudgsicle away from him before frostbite set in.

Andy had a lack of knowledge. He was too young to grasp the concept of holding a wooden stick to save his fingers from the cold. His lack of knowledge cost him painful fingers and prevented him from finishing the rest of his yummy Fudgsicle. Even though Mommy and Grandma tried to help him, he was so focused on what he wanted that he couldn't see what was hurting him, so he refused our help. I wonder how many times we've all lacked knowledge in a situation and kicked and screamed when God tried to help us. Just like Andy, we all want to do things our own way—even though it hurts us—all because we lack knowledge.

For more insight, let's look at our scripture in the context it was written in. The Bible says in Hosea 4:6, "My people are destroyed for a lack of knowledge." The people had a lack of knowledge because the priests had not taught them as God instructed them to. God was quite upset with the priests for their failure to properly teach his people. With no knowledge of God's Word, the people soon turned to idol worship.

The priests failed to teach, and their neglect led to the destruction of the people. Perhaps your trial is a result of a lack of knowledge because you weren't properly taught. Let me make something very clear: not being taught is only a part of the problem. At some point, we all must take personal responsibility for our actions, whether we've been taught right or not. There's no playing the blame game when it comes to our own sin.

God holds people accountable for what they are responsible to teach. As parents, we are responsible to teach our children about God and to raise them up with good morals and integrity. It's then their responsibility to walk in the right way.

The same thing applies to pastors, who are also held accountable for what they teach their congregations. If a pastor waters down the Word of God to satisfy a lazy congregation, God notices. The congregation that is not taught the Word of God correctly is more apt to wander away into sin—or stay there if they're in blatant sin already. But when a pastor teaches the hard truths of God's Word for the benefit of his congregation, God is pleased and the congregation at least has knowledge. It's then up to them whether or not they apply it. But without knowledge, the people will be destroyed in some area of their lives.

The following is a scenario that describes perishing due to a lack of knowledge. Suppose you are in a serious relationship and are contemplating marriage. Let's say your parents had a terrible marriage; your church doesn't counsel couples before marrying them; your pastor doesn't preach from the pulpit the specific roles God has assigned for married men and women; you haven't searched the Scriptures yourself to discover God's plan for marriage; and you haven't read Christian books on marriage. You will have a lack of knowledge, and a stormy marriage is likely in the forecast for you. Sound like a bad confession? The sad fact is, most people just don't know how to be happily married, and the divorce rate in the church proves it. This lack of knowledge brings destruction.

Another example of a lack of knowledge is in the area of finances. Few people these days are taught how to manage their money according to God's Word. If they don't know to tithe, give offerings, save, and live within their means, they soon find themselves drowning in debt. The average Joe and Jane Christian just don't know what they're doing financially—because they've never been taught. The result is stress and strain and often, divorce.

So take a look at your trial and see if the root of it is a lack of knowledge. If it is, look in God's Word for the knowledge you need. Seek out people who will give godly counsel and turn your trial around. Refuse to let a lack of knowledge destroy you again. Andy eventually learned to hold the stick, and you can too!

SOME TRIALS COME BECAUSE SATAN IS TRYING TO STEAL, KILL, OR DESTROY

The thief does not come except to steal, and to kill, and to destroy.

John 10:10

Identity theft—we're warned about it every day. We must carefully guard our private information from the criminals who want to steal from us. The problem with identity theft is that the victim doesn't realize he's a victim until it's too late. In the good ol' days, the thief picked your pocket and got away with a little bit of cash. Today, he steals your credit card information and shops 'til he drops, making the next several years of your life miserable as you try to clean up your credit record.

Satan is like the identity thief. He doesn't want you to realize that he's stealing from you until he's stolen all you've got. He wants to sneak into your life and take from you until he utterly destroys you. He uses many avenues to achieve his wicked purposes. He may bring a person into your life who tempts you to live in bitterness, unforgiveness, or offense. He may tempt you with an addiction that will rob you of your health and all your relationships. He may whisper in your ear and convince you that you are too unworthy to serve the Lord. All of these attempts will rob you of the abundant life Jesus wants you to live.

Open your eyes and see if your trial is a result of Satan's attempt to steal, kill, or destroy you. If you discern that it is, there's no need to fear; the Scriptures tell us how to gain victory in our battles with this enemy, and they are discussed in my book *Trials: Now What?*

Are you on fire for the Lord and growing spiritually every day? Welcome to target practice—for Satan—because you've got a big target on your back! Anyone on the move toward a closer walk with God is just who Satan will be gunning for—and perhaps that explains your trial. He wants to thwart your spiritual growth. Jesus gave the explanation of the parable of the Sower in Matthew 13. In that passage, there's a phrase that could easily be overlooked but holds a truth we need to see.

> But he who received the seed on stony places, this is he who hears the word and immediately receives it with joy; yet he has no root in himself, but endures only for a while. For when tribulation or persecution arises because of the word, immediately he stumbles.
>
> Matthew 13:20–21

Forget for a moment the condition of the receiver, and notice why the tribulation and persecution came—because of the word. When the person heard the Word, Satan sprang into action, sending tribulation and persecution, trying to prevent the Word from taking root. And the person in this case—who had gladly heard and received the Word in the beginning—was too spiritually shallow and stumbled at the tribulation.

Satan is out to stop anyone in any spiritual condition from letting God's Word have an impact on his or her life. His tactics include everything from persecution to distraction. Satan is our enemy, and he doesn't fight fair. But we have weapons of warfare to fight back that are much more powerful than anything Satan can do to us.

> Nor give place to the devil.
>
> Ephesians 4:27

Satan indeed tries to destroy us with sneak attacks. At other times, we are just plain negligent in protecting our own spiritual house and we leave a door wide open for him to waltz right in—we've given place to the devil. Perhaps your trial is a result of an open door—like anger—where you let the devil in, and once he was comfortably situated inside, he began his methodical destruction in your life. Search for those open doors and lock them up.

SOME TRIALS COME BECAUSE THE WORLD HATES YOU

If the world hates you, you know that it hated Me before it hated you. If you were of the world, the world would love its own. Yet because you are not of the world, but I chose you out of the world, therefore the world hates you. Remember the word that I said to you, "A servant is not greater than his master." If they persecuted Me, they will also persecute you.

John 15:18–20

We all want to be liked. Some may boast that they don't care what anybody thinks of them, but seldom is that really the truth. But there comes a time in the life of a Christian when he or she will have to choose between being liked and standing for Christ. Choosing to stand for Christ may bring you a trial.

I sold door-to-door cosmetics when I was in my twenties. Living in a small town, I knew most of my customers well and interacted with them in various community groups. While delivering an order to a customer one day, she and I had a conversation that led to the topic of abortion. I commented on how I believed abortion took the life of an innocent child. I was naïve enough to think that anyone who lived in rural Oklahoma—the Bible belt, for goodness' sake—would agree with me. She did not. Her snappy response to my comment was close to hostile. Needless to say, that was the end of her cosmetic orders. To complicate matters, she and I were involved in an upcoming community event where she had ample opportunity to make me miserable, and she did. As far as I know, I was persecuted for no reason other than my belief and my refusal to back down when she disagreed with me. Despite my hurt feelings, I survived the episode just fine, and I have no animosity toward this woman. But I discovered what Jesus meant by the world hating me because it hates him. The hostility directed toward me in this story pales in comparison to those dear saints who've suffered severe hardship and even martyrdom for the cause of Christ.

Maybe your trial is the result of a stand you took for Christ.

Taking a stand for him will cost you every time. Oh, there may be a few who quietly admire your conviction and courage, but few will stand beside you. Many people just don't want to rock the boat. They don't want to suffer the repercussions, they aren't really sure what they believe, or they want to go along to get along. When you find yourself in any degree of persecution, perhaps utterly alone, remember that Jesus walked this road before you and he will supply all the grace you need to faithfully endure.

GOD IS SOVEREIGN IN YOUR TRIAL

God is sovereign. Most people have heard this statement, but many may not be exactly sure what it means. The church is famous for using phrases like this and assuming everyone knows what they mean. Some newer Bible translations use *sovereign* to describe God. Older translations use terms like *the Most High God* or *the Lord God* where the newer translations insert the word *sovereign*. When we look for the definition of *sovereign*, we find words and phrases like, *supreme authority, none higher, permanent authority*. Many people find it easy to believe that God is the supreme authority and that God is in control. But the real nitty-gritty questions they struggle with are "How involved is God in the details of my everyday life"? and "What exactly does God control or allow?" Those are the type of questions people debate.

There tend to be two extremes when people discuss the sovereignty of God. One opinion is fatalistic and believes that it doesn't matter what you do, we're basically puppets in the hand of God, and we have no control over what ultimately happens in our lives. The other opinion is that we are totally in control of every event that happens in our lives—because God has given us dominion—and if something bad has happened, it's a result of a lack of faith or we've failed to take authority over the situation. I believe the truth is found in a balance between these two opposing thoughts.

I believe God does orchestrate some circumstances in our lives to carry out his purpose, which is to use us for his glory. He is so much higher than we are that while in our mortal bodies, we will never fully comprehend all his ways. However, I also find in the Scriptures that Jesus has transferred authority to us, but not to the degree that we neglect or disobey the one who is the supreme authority and ignore the one who is in complete control. I believe in complete surrender to the will of God, understanding that even if he leads me down a difficult path, it's ultimately for my own good and his glory. I also know that Satan wants to destroy me and when he tries to harm me I should exercise my God-given authority over him as the Holy Spirit directs—all while trusting God to work everything out for my own good.

I believe God's plan is to bring me into a closer, more intimate knowledge of him, and only he knows what avenues will get me there. Of course, he has given me free will, and he will not override it. I have the option to reject him, but once I willingly give him my heart and accept his salvation, then I have chosen him as the Lord of my life. Because I've given myself to him, he can use whatever pressures are necessary to bring me back to him if I start to wander away from him. If he allows me to be hurt in the process, he'll tend my wounds with loving care.

So when a trial comes into my life, I am thankful for God's sovereignty, and even when I may not understand why the trial has come, I trust his love for me no matter what I face. We are by no means puppets, but God does have a master plan for each of our lives. Unless you are rebelling at every turn, he will put you where he wants you. On this subject, David wrote in a psalm that it is God who directs the steps of a good man.

> The steps of a good man are ordered by the Lord, and He delights in his way. Though he fall, he shall not be utterly cast down; For the Lord upholds him with His hand.
>
> Psalm 37:23–24

David points out that the Lord directs the steps of a good man, and when that man falls, the Lord will uphold him. The word translated as *uphold* means to "prop up." If I prop up something, it's because it can't stay upright by itself. So the word picture here seems to be that God leads us along a path, we fall down for any variety of reasons, but we can trust that the Lord will prop us back up and direct our steps from there.

God, in his sovereignty, may allow difficulties in our lives to make us better or move us to a different place. Consider how a spring storm naturally prunes away branches from trees and scatters seeds to new fields. At first glance, a violent windstorm appears to have brought destruction, as tree limbs are scattered about. But when the results are examined in the later months, the trained eye can see new, stronger, and more fruitful growth emerging where old, dead, useless, and weak branches were blown away. If the careful observer widens his view, he will see new seedlings sprouting up because seeds were carried in the wind from the storm-tossed tree—new life, in a new place, as a result of a storm.

> Therefore, let those who suffer according to the will of God commit their souls to Him in doing good, as to a faithful Creator.
>
> 1 Peter 4:19

According to Rick Renner in *Sparkling Gems from the Greek,* the word translated as *suffer* means "to suffer as a result of outside forces or outside circumstances." Thinking about trials that cause you to suffer, you'll realize that many of them are from outside forces and leave you little control over the situation. Now look at the next phrase from 1 Peter 4:19: "according to the will of God." This phrase cannot be ignored, and we must assume that when outside pressures are upon us, it is because God has allowed them—he is sovereign. Continuing on in the same verse, we find the phrase, "commit their souls to Him." Read what *The Wycliffe Bible Commentary* says on this phrase.

19. Let them that suffer…commit. Let them rest their case with their Maker, even as did Christ (2:23). To do so betokens the calmness of that divinely implanted love that casts out fear (cf. 1 Jn 4:18).

Now let's apply the thoughts from these three phrases to your trial and the sovereignty of God. First of all, you find yourself suffering due to some pressure from the outside. It could be physical, mental, spiritual, or financial—and you have practically no control to change it. This has come upon you because it's passed through the sovereign hand of God; he has allowed it for some purpose that is likely not apparent to you now. Your response should be to rest your case with God and calmly trust him to work it out for your good.

In the same vein, in *My Utmost for His Highest*, Oswald Chambers comments,

> Do we not see God at work in our circumstances? Dark times are allowed and come to us through the sovereignty of God. Are we prepared to let God do what He wants with us? Are we prepared to be separated from the outward, evident blessings of God? Until Jesus Christ is truly our Lord, we each have goals of our own which we serve. Our faith is real, but it is not yet permanent. And God is never in a hurry. If we are willing to wait, we will see God pointing out that we have been interested only in His blessings, instead of in God Himself.

It's the sovereignty and the love of God that allows us to go through trials, all for a purpose. The purpose is to make our faith real and permanent—not shallow and weak—and to bring us into an intimate knowledge of God. It's the same principle as the storm pruning away dead or weak branches in a storm—they must be removed for stronger growth and fruit to come. When we truly grasp this concept, we can calmly surrender our all to our sovereign God in any storm.

In *My Utmost for His Highest*, Oswald Chambers goes on to further say, "A saint realizes that it is God who engineers his circumstances; consequently there are no complaints, only unrestrained surrender to Jesus."

When will we realize the weakness of our flesh? Without the intervention of God in our everyday circumstances, we would only have a superficial relationship with the Lord—wanting only what he can give us, and never giving ourselves in return. We would remain in an immature state spiritually and suffer greater loss as we lived our lives without an intimate walk with God. But when God allows the storm to come, our thankful eyes are opened to our heavenly Father to make us know him—and in a deeper way than we could have known him before the violent winds.

Another comment from Oswald Chambers in *My Utmost for His Highest* says,

> If you yourself do not cut the lines that tie you to the dock, God will have to use a storm to sever them and to send you out to sea. Put everything in your life afloat upon God, going out to sea on the great swelling tide of His purpose, and your eyes will be opened. If you believe in Jesus, you are not to spend all your time in the calm waters just inside the harbor, full of joy, but always tied to the dock. You have to get out past the harbor into the great depths of God, and begin to know things for yourself—begin to have spiritual discernment.

So, as our brother Chambers so eloquently puts it in his commentary, God uses a storm to bring us into his purpose for us, into greater spiritual insight, and most importantly, a more intimate knowledge of him.

Paul wrote to the Corinthian church about the experience of trials and the results they bring. *The Message Bible* translates it as follows:

> We've been surrounded and battered by troubles, but we're not demoralized; we're not sure what to do, but we know that God knows what to do; we've been spiritually terrorized, but God hasn't left our side; we've been thrown down, but we haven't broken.

What they did to Jesus, they do to us—trial and torture, mockery and murder; what Jesus did among them, He does in us—He lives! Our lives are at constant risk for Jesus' sake, which makes Jesus' life all the more evident in us. While we're going through the worst, you're getting in on the best!

We're not keeping this quiet, not on your life. Just like the psalmist who wrote, "I believed it, so I said it," we say what we believe. And what we believe is that the One who raised up the Master Jesus will just as certainly raise us up with you, alive. Every detail works to your advantage and to God's glory: more and more grace, more and more people, more and more praise!

So we're not giving up. How could we! Even though on the outside it often looks like things are falling apart on us, on the inside, where God is making new life, not a day goes by without his unfolding grace. These hard times are small potatoes compared to the coming good times, the lavish celebration prepared for us. There's far more here than meets the eye. The things we see now are here today, gone tomorrow. But the things we can't see now will last forever.

2 Corinthians 4:8–18 (MSG)

Paul expresses that no matter how bad our trials are, God, who is sovereign, is doing a work in them, and it will work out for our good and his glory. Oh, be thankful that our good God doesn't waste even our worst days. He can recycle any windblown branch into a thing of beauty, bursting forth with the evidence of new life, when it's placed in his hands.

God allows some circumstances in our lives; others are his sovereign hand orchestrating them. Because God's people repeatedly disobeyed him, he allowed them to be carried away by their enemies and spend seventy years as captives in Babylon. Then their sovereign God orchestrated the conquering of the Babylonians by Cyrus, king of Persia. God performed another sovereign act when he moved upon the pagan heart of Cyrus and caused him to not only free the Jews, but to give them money to go home and rebuild their city.

> Now in the first year of Cyrus king of Persia, that the word of the Lord spoken by the mouth of Jeremiah might be fulfilled, the Lord stirred up the spirit of Cyrus king of Persia, so that he made a proclamation, throughout all his kingdom, and also put it in writing, saying, "Thus says Cyrus king of Persia: 'All the kingdoms of the earth the Lord God of heaven has given me. And He has commanded me to build Him a house at Jerusalem which is in Judah. Who is there among you of all His people? May the Lord his God be with him, and let him go up!'"
>
> 2 Chronicles 36:22–23

Long before God's people were led away in chains and fetters to Babylon, Isaiah prophesied all the details of this very event. He even noted the name of Cyrus, before he was king of Persia, who would be used as a tool in the sovereign hand of God. In the next four passages listed from Isaiah 45, God tells the sequence of events many years before they take place.

> Thus says the Lord to His anointed, to Cyrus, whose right hand I have held—to subdue nations before him and loose the armor of kings …
>
> Isaiah 45:1

God raised up Cyrus as king of Persia to subdue the Babylonians, who had destroyed Jerusalem and taken God's people captive.

> I have named you, though you have not known Me.
>
> Isaiah 45:4

God named Cyrus and used him to deliver God's people, even though Cyrus was a pagan and did not know Jehovah God as the one true God.

> I am the Lord, and there is no other; there is no God besides Me. I will gird you, though you have not known Me, that they may know from the rising of the sun to its setting that there is none

besides me. I am the Lord, and there is no other; I form the light and create darkness, I make peace and create calamity; I, the Lord, do all these things.

Isaiah 45:5–7

Although King Cyrus of Persia was a pagan man who did not know God, God still used him to accomplish his purposes. In the passage above, we need to understand why God says he makes peace and he creates calamity. God is forever sovereign, and he allowed the Babylonians to carry away his people, but it was a result of their own sin and rebellion against God. We must know that God never orchestrates sin; mankind alone is responsible for sin and its consequences. When God says he brings calamity, he is not saying he orchestrates sinful acts. Rather, any calamity God allows has a purpose to ultimately bring peace and spiritual growth to at least a faithful remnant of his people.

> "I have raised him up in righteousness, and I will direct all his ways; He shall build My city and let My exiles go free, not for price nor reward," says the Lord of hosts.
>
> Isaiah 45:13

Even though it made no earthly sense for him to do so, Cyrus let God's exiled people return to Jerusalem. God's people knowingly sinned and rebelled against him—their own free will choice. Yet God allowed their captivity and orchestrated their return for the greater purpose of a remnant of his people emerging from the trial stronger—full of faith—and blessed by the almighty, sovereign hand of God.

While God's people were still in captivity in Babylon, their idol-worshiping captors probably mocked the weakness of their God, laughing at his failure to protect them. The mocking crowd would soon discover what the psalmist already knew.

> Not unto us, O Lord, not unto us, but to Your name give glory, because of Your mercy, and because of Your truth. Why should the

Gentiles say, "Where now is their God?" But our God is in heaven; He does whatever He pleases.

Psalm 115:1–3

When the crowd around you sees you in the midst of your trial they too may ask, "Where is the God you serve?" Your response should be similar to how the psalmist answered back then. "What happens to me doesn't matter, as long as God gets glory. If God allows me to experience difficult circumstances, it's all for a holy purpose."

And we know that all things work together for good to those who love God, to those who are the called according to His purpose. For whom He foreknew, He also predestined to be conformed to the image of His Son, that He might be the firstborn among many brethren.

Romans 8:28–29

God's plan and purpose for each of his children is conforming them into the image of his Son. He will allow and orchestrate events in their lives to bring them to this destination of Christlikeness. He is never responsible for sin. He does not override our free will choices, but he can be very effective in his persuasion. As Oral Roberts said so often, "God is a good God." His goodness and his sovereignty will always be for our ultimate good.

We cannot study the sovereignty of God without looking at the story of Joseph. Joseph's life was like a yo-yo—up and down, up and down. The book of Genesis records the dramatic chain of events. Joseph was his father's favorite son, and his jealous brothers conspired to kill him. Deciding to make a profit instead, they sold young Joseph into slavery. The upside was that upon being bought in Egypt, Joseph the slave was soon promoted in his master's house. Things turned downward when he rejected his master's wife's sexual advances, and in her scorn, she falsely accused him of attempted rape. That resulted in a dreadful prison sentence. But things were back on the upward swing when God gave Joseph favor in the eyes of the prison keeper, who quickly promoted Joseph within the prison system. Joseph later correctly interpreted two dreams while in prison, hoping it would lead to his freedom, but on the downside again, he was not remembered and remained in prison for two more years. When Pharaoh had a disturbing dream, Joseph was called upon to interpret it, which he did, and that prompted his release from prison. He was immediately put in charge of all Egypt, answering only to Pharaoh himself. Bear in mind that all these traumatic ups and downs occurred in Joseph's life before he had turned thirty years old.

When a widespread famine came upon the land, Joseph's family, back home in Canaan, was desperate for food and traveled to Egypt to purchase it. God had given Joseph supernatural knowledge and wisdom that caused him to store enough grain in preparation for the famine. The up and down paths of Joseph's tragic and blessed life put him in the ideal place for God to reunite the entire family and preserve the lineage of Jesus. Joseph recognized the sovereign hand of God in every single detail of his up-and-down life when he spoke to his brothers—whom he had tearfully forgiven.

> And God sent me before you to preserve a posterity for you in the earth, and to save your lives by a great deliverance. So now it was not you who sent me here, but God; and He has made me a father to Pharaoh, and lord of all his house, and a ruler throughout all the land of Egypt.
>
> Genesis 45:7–8

> But as for you, you meant evil against me; but God meant it for good, in order to bring it about as it is this day, to save many people alive.
>
> Genesis 50:20

The psalmist recounted Joseph's story and spoke of God's sovereignty and testing of Joseph. He pointed out that it was God who called for the famine and destroyed their provision of bread, and it was also God who sent deliverance for his people through Joseph and the circumstances that placed him second in command over all Egypt.

God had a plan and a purpose for Joseph and his people—and he was always in control.

> Moreover He called for a famine in the land; He destroyed all the provision of bread. He sent a man before them—Joseph—who was sold as a slave. They hurt his feet with fetters, he was laid in irons. Until the time that his word came to pass, the word of the Lord tested him.
>
> Psalm 105:16–19

Beth Moore eloquently stated on James Robison's *Life Today* TV program, "If the purpose doesn't exceed the pain, God will not allow it." She was referring to the sovereignty of God and went on to explain that we must cooperate with God's plan, or we will be left with the pain and miss out on the purpose.

If Joseph had failed any of the tests in his yo-yo life, the story may have had an entirely different ending. But Joseph did right by his masters. He didn't worship idols when his peers did. He fled from a seducing woman. He told the truth about the dreams he interpreted. He didn't harbor unforgiveness against his brothers, the woman who falsely accused him, or the former prisoners who forgot him. Above all, he stayed faithful to God, who used Joseph's pain for his sovereign purpose. We can trust—and be thankful for—the sovereign hand of God.

GOD IS SOVEREIGN IN HIS JUDGMENT

All I had left to do was mop the kitchen floor and I could finally sit down for a few minutes, watch some afternoon television, and enjoy a drink and a cookie. I had just put the last chair upside down on the kitchen table—clearing the floor below for easy mopping—when I saw Janie standing in the kitchen entry.

Our house was barely one thousand square feet, and the entry into our country kitchen was no wider than a doorway. It was time for our afternoon snack, and she wanted a drink and a cookie. I explained to her that we would have our snack together when I finished mopping. She didn't seem to mind waiting for the snack, but at three years old, she was still intrigued with the chore of mopping and putting her feet on a wet floor. I made it perfectly clear to her that she needed to stay out of the kitchen while I mopped, and I pointed out the threshold of the kitchen where living room carpet met wood-look kitchen vinyl. She completely understood the directions I gave her: "Stay on the carpet; do not step on the vinyl floor."

I pushed the mop back and forth across the vinyl floor until the mop needed to be wrung out. When I turned toward my mop bucket, there stood my cute little girl in her yellow Tweety Bird sweat suit with one arm on the door trim, one foot on the carpet—where she was supposed to be—and the other foot planted firmly on the vinyl floor, and two big blue eyes looking straight at me to see what I would do. She was in complete and total defiance. She disobeyed a direct order, which she perfectly understood, and she was testing—perhaps even daring me—to do something about it.

The day had been going so well. I didn't *plan* to spank her that day. I didn't want an excuse to spank her. Her own free will choice forced me to discipline her. I was the momma, I was in control, I was sovereign in my house, and I loved her enough to stop her defiant behavior. I spanked. She cried. I sat down and had my snack. She sat in her room without one. Lesson learned.

Janie's original plan was to just come get juice and a cookie, which I was happy to get for her on my own time. She was distracted by a shiny floor and tempted to touch it. Disobedience cost Janie a drink of juice, a cookie, and fellowship with Mommy for a little while.

God loves his children more than you and I love our own. He will discipline and judge, and he will be sovereign in the way he does it. Let's look at the story of King Solomon. Solomon was the son of King David and he loved God. First Kings 3 records how Solomon asked God for an understanding heart—what we would call wisdom. God was so pleased with Solomon's unselfish request that he granted him the wisdom he asked for, along with great wealth and honor. Solomon later built the magnificent temple in Jerusalem, the first permanent house of God.

When the temple was completed, the Lord appeared to Solomon. God gave Solomon a warning, which is recorded in First Kings 9. The short version of this warning is that God promised blessings for obedience to him and calamity for disobedience. Disobedience would include going after other gods and worshiping them, and God made that warning very plain.

During his reign, Solomon acquired riches and fame—and foreign wives. God specifically instructed his people not to marry idol worshipers. It's not that God doesn't love all people—we know he does—but the foreigners brought their idolatrous ways into the homes of God's people and influenced them against the Lord God. That is exactly what happened to Solomon. First Kings 11 lists the wives of King Solomon—not by name, but by number! He had seven hundred wives, princesses, and three hundred concubines. He had intimate contact with all these idol-worshiping women, and because of their strong influence on him, Solomon's heart soon turned away from the Lord God. He even built altars for their foreign idols and eventually worshiped them himself.

> For it was so, when Solomon was old, that his wives turned his heart after other gods; and his heart was not loyal to the Lord his God, as was the heart of his father David. For Solomon went after Ashtoreth the goddess of the Sidonians, and after Milcom the abomination of the Ammonites. Then Solomon built a high place for Chemosh the abomination of Moab, on the hill that is east of Jerusalem, and for Molech the abomination of the people of Ammon. So the Lord became angry with Solomon, because his heart had turned from the Lord God of Israel, who had appeared to him twice and had commanded him concerning this thing, that he should not go after other gods; but he did not keep what the Lord had commanded.
>
> 1 Kings 11:4–5, 7, 9–10

There was no failure to communicate between God and Solomon. God appeared to this man twice! God, knowing Solomon's weakness, specifically instructed him to not go after foreign gods. Solomon did it anyway. The sovereign God, like any good parent, could not ignore direct disobedience. God's judgment would tear the kingdom away from Solomon and give it to a servant. But even in the judgment, God showed mercy and said he would delay this event until the reign of Solomon's son. God was also merciful when he promised not to tear away the entire kingdom. He allowed the tribe of Judah to remain under the reign of Solomon's family. Directly after speaking this judgment to Solomon, God made a sovereign move.

> Now the Lord raised up an adversary against Solomon, Hadad the Edomite.
>
> 1 Kings 11:14

And God raised up another adversary against him, Rezon the son of Eliadah.

1 Kings 11:23

Then Solomon's servant, Jeroboam the son of Nebat, an Ephraimite from Zereda, whose mother's name was Zeruah, a widow, also rebelled against the king.

1 Kings 11:26

Solomon and his kingdom suddenly have three sets of adversaries. Plots thicken and the story unfolds, but to make a long story short, Solomon dies and his son Rehoboam is made king. Ten tribes of Israel rebel and form a country separate from King Rehoboam. Rehoboam assembles an army to try to restore his father's kingdom. Before the army can leave, a man of God speaks these solemn words to Rehoboam:

Thus says the Lord: "You shall not go up nor fight against your brethren the children of Israel. Let every man return to his house, for this thing is from Me."

1 Kings 12:24

Notice that God said, "This thing is from me." God, in his sovereignty, ripped apart Solomon's kingdom. Did God want to? No! It wasn't his original plan. Solomon's willful and continued sin forced the entire situation. Just like my daughter, Solomon didn't plan to sin, but he was distracted by his wives and knowingly yielded to the temptation to worship idols. God doesn't enjoy seeing us in painful trials. When our own sinful choices initiate them, he is always just and always sovereign—totally in control—even when we are not. God does enjoy what a painful trial has the potential to produce—a repentant heart that loves the Lord and seeks the face of God.

Solomon started off with a heart that loved the Lord. Then he wed that first foreign bride; he must have rationalized in his mind that one beautiful idol-worshiping woman would not be so bad! But it was a sin; he excused it, he rationalized it, and soon he became so numb to it that he became an idol worshiper himself. Therein lays the danger of sin. At some point we get so used to it that we don't even recognize that it is sin anymore.

As Christians today, we must guard our own hearts against the same slippery slope of ignoring a sin in our lives and letting it continue. Even though Jesus has saved us from the eternal penalty of sin, we will still give an account for our sins as Paul clearly taught the Corinthians.

> Therefore we make it our aim, whether present or absent, to be well pleasing to Him. For we must all appear before the judgment seat of Christ, that each one may receive the things done in the body, according to what he has done, whether good or bad.
>
> 2 Corinthians 5:9–10

God is full of grace and mercy, yet he is holy and just. He cannot overlook willful sin. He can forgive it—most surely. But we'll all give an account to the supreme authority, our sovereign God.

GOD WANTS YOU TO FINISH WELL

Being confident of this very thing, that He who has begun a good work in you will complete it until the day of Jesus Christ...

Philippians 1:6

One day, my husband, Buddy, walked into the house after his drive home from work and exclaimed, "Your flowers look really good! I noticed them as soon as I turned the corner onto our street!" We walked back outdoors together to admire the sea of white petunias—which did look fabulous, if I must say so myself! I led him over to the flower bed and said, "Watch me; this is why my flowers are full of blooms." I bent down and carefully pinched off baby flower buds, explaining to Buddy that only gardeners with the guts to prune get blooms like mine.

Pruning was a hard concept for me to grasp when I first began gardening. I wanted instant gratification, and I wanted every bud to bloom. But as I found the courage to prune my flowers and shrubs, I learned that the payoff was worth the temporary pain. There are rules to pruning, and I'm still learning them. Some plants can be sheared back at anytime. With others, if you prune the wrong branch at the wrong time, you'll ruin next season's blooms. A master gardener knows these things; I'm still a novice. But when it comes to petunias, I know what needs to be done to have the showiest blooms on the street!

We live on a busy neighborhood street in friendly, small-town Oklahoma where even a stranger will still smile and wave at you. It makes my day when I'm working outside and a car stops so the driver can compliment me on how pretty my flowers are. But not one person has ever walked up to the petunias and said, "My, you look so pretty!" They give the compliments to me! I'm the one who planted them in the right place, gave them water and fertilizer, and pruned them when they needed it. The petunias by themselves might look okay for a brief time, but eventually end up with long, leggy stems, dried brown leaves, and only a few blooms. But in the hand of a gardener who knows just what they need, they become a sight to behold.

God is your Master Gardener, and he knows just what you need to make you the kind of Christian that will bring him glory when people look at you. He knows what city, job, family, or church you need to be planted in. He knows when you need to be painfully pruned and exactly how it should be done. The purpose of the pruning is always for your own good and his glory. Pruning will force you to send your roots deeper into him. It will also get rid of your weak branches—whatever that may be in your life—so they won't drain energy away from the good ones. And most importantly, pruning will make you bear more fruit. In the end, you are a sight to behold!

> I am the true vine, and My Father is the vinedresser. Every branch in Me that does not bear fruit He takes away; and every branch that bears fruit He prunes, that it may bear more fruit.
>
> John 15:1–2

Is the Master Gardener pruning you? I hope he is! It's probably gonna hurt a little—well, maybe a lot—but wait until you see what it produces in you. Remember, the spiritual pruning process is all for a good purpose. You go through hard times—pruning—and your character improves. Maybe you become gentler or more patient. Perhaps your pruning results in you becoming a kinder, more peaceful person because of the perspective you'll gain in your trial. Could it be that your pruning might force you to take control of a weakness in your flesh? The result of your pruning is more fruit—as in the fruit of the Spirit. There's a big difference between gifts and fruit. God gives us spiritual gifts. He doesn't give us fruit; he tends us and prunes us until it's developed over time. Oh, be thankful for a Master Gardener and his tender pruning hand that causes you to bear much fruit.

> But the fruit of the Spirit is love, joy, peace, longsuffering, kindness, goodness, faithfulness, gentleness, self-control.
>
> Galatians 5:22–23

Oswald Chambers, in *My Utmost for His Highest,* said,

> The greatest difficulty spiritually is to concentrate on God, and His blessings are what make it so difficult. Troubles almost always make us look to God, but His blessings tend to divert our attention elsewhere.

How true! We know God wants us to live an abundant life. But when God blesses us and we get more enamored with the blessings than with him, we aren't living in abundance. When everything is peachy keen in our lives, the temptation is to get spiritually lazy—the prayer life and Bible study start to fade away in our comfortable state. Compare the comfortable person with the person going through the toughest trial of her life. Which one is daily on her knees, desperate for the presence of God? Which one is daily searching the Word of God for solutions and answers, a word from God, or comfort? It could and should be both people, but most often, it's only the one in trouble. So could some troubles actually be for our good? I think so! God loves us too much to leave us the way we are—spiritually lazy.

I was teaching on this topic in Sunday school when my friend commented, "What you're really saying is 'A fat dog won't hunt!'" That was exactly right! Give a hound dog pup too much food and no training, and he'll just lay contentedly in the shade of the porch.

Why should he learn to hunt? All his needs are met, but he'll be of no use to his master. On the other hand, if that same hound dog pup gets the right amount of food, exercise, and training every day, he'll eagerly put his nose to the ground, learn to obey his master, and ultimately make his master proud.

In simple terms, here's what we need to remember: God is a good God, and no one on this earth loves us more than he does. No one wants the best for us more than he does. No one but he knows what is best for us. God wants us to finish well, and he will complete the good work he has started in us.

God has done his fair share of pruning in my life, and I'm thankful for it. I'm better than I was, but I'm not content to stay the way I am. I want to be a more fruitful Christian and more Christlike. As much as I want to keep progressing in my spiritual journey, God desires it even more for me. He wants me to be one with him. Once again, Oswald Chambers gives insight into this subject in *My Utmost for His Highest* when he says,

> God always ignores your present level of completeness in favor of your ultimate future completeness. He is not concerned about making you blessed and happy right now, but He's continually working out His ultimate perfection for you—"…that they may be one just as We are one" John 17:22

I guess we could say God is a perfectionist—he wants to bring us into perfection. The journey to that perfection begins with grace; God wants us no matter how dirty, broken, or sin stained our lives may be. His goal is to take our soiled lives and polish us until every little part of us sparkles and shines. He loves and accepts us no matter what condition we're in, but he loves us too much to leave us in our sad and pitiful condition once the blood of his Son has redeemed us. He won't completely finish this perfection process until we shed our bodies of flesh. That's when he will finally present us to his Son as the spotless, perfect bride of Christ. But until then, our loving God will keep scrutinizing our every flaw—lovingly dealing with us through the Holy Spirit to let him change us. Our job is to cooperate with his process. He wants us to recognize our own ugly nature and allow him to polish—or prune—that ugliness away. The methods he chooses are up to him. His ways are higher than our ways, and we just have to trust him when we can't explain a trial. We must be thankful when we find ourselves being pruned, scrubbed, or polished by the Master's hand.

GOD IS NOT MEAN AND DOESN'T ENJOY SEEING YOU SUFFER

For thus says the Lord: After seventy years are completed at Babylon, I will visit you and perform My good word toward you, and cause you to return to this place. For I know the thoughts that I think toward you, says the Lord, thoughts of peace and not of evil, to give you a future and a hope.

Jeremiah 29:10–11

Before going any farther, let me explain the context of the verse above. God's people were stiff-necked and rebellious toward him. He warned them multiple times through his prophets, but they refused to stay true to the Lord. Finally, in judgment, God allowed the Babylonians—also called the Chaldeans—to conquer them and carry them away in captivity. The Prophet Jeremiah spoke the Word of the Lord by way of a letter to the people who were in captivity in Babylon, and that is recorded above from Jeremiah 29.

Notice the mercy in God's wording as he speaks to them while they are suffering in this time of judgment on their nation's sin. God first makes clear in verse ten that they have to endure seventy full years of captivity. Then he promised to visit them and perform his good word toward them and bring them home. Nowhere does it mention the condition of their hearts at this point—God is always the initiator of grace and mercy to his people. God further tells them that the thoughts he thinks toward them are thoughts of peace and not of evil. God also promised them hope in their future, indicating that God is most interested in the final outcome. The proof of this was written several chapters earlier in the same book of Jeremiah.

> Thus says the Lord, the God of Israel: "Like these good figs, so will I acknowledge those who are carried away captive from Judah, whom I have sent out of this place for their own good, into the land of the Chaldeans. For I will set My eyes on them for good, and I will bring them back to this land; I will build them and not pull them down, and I will plant them and not pluck them up. Then I will give them a heart to know Me, that I am the Lord; and they shall be My people, and I will be their God, for they shall return to Me with their whole heart."
>
> Jeremiah 24:5–7

God responded to the sin of his people by orchestrating a judgment that wasn't meant to punish them as much as it was meant to turn them. Notice that God says his eyes are on them for good and he is the one who—through the difficult circumstances—gives them a heart to know him.

It's always God who ultimately does the good work in us; we certainly aren't capable of doing it without his help! Paul wrote to the Ephesians that we are his workmanship. Read below from the Amplified Bible and pay close attention to the statement about our paths.

> For we are God's [own] handiwork (His workmanship), recreated in Christ Jesus, [born anew] that we may do those good works which God predestined (planned beforehand) for us [taking paths which He prepared ahead of time], that we should walk in them [living the good life which He prearranged and made ready for us to live].
>
> Ephesians 2:10 (AMP)

Anything good in us is a result of a work God has done in us—we are his workmanship. Obviously, we have to cooperate to some degree, but only he can take the credit for what we become, for it is he who has even prepared the paths we take in life. Again, we see the sovereignty of God. God is making it so clear that he wants only the best for his people; he wants us to live the good life! He thinks thoughts for our peace, our best welfare, and he never does us harm or evil. A typical response to that statement would be, "Then explain my trial!" The answer to that question begins with another question: "Is an explanation really necessary?" Whatever your trial is, whatever has produced it, in the end all that really matters is that God wants the best for you, and that includes knowing him better than you do today. Your trial can lead you closer to the Lord or pull you farther away from him. That choice is completely yours.

The hurting heart struggles to see past the immediate pain, and we've all been in those shoes at some time or another. Many of us have shaken our fists at God—or at least thought about it—when our pain was so great and we couldn't make sense of the tragedy surrounding us. Let's look at a family who went through those same heartrending emotions.

Lazarus and his two sisters, Martha and Mary, were close friends of Jesus. Jesus had been a guest in their home on at least one occasion. Lazarus became very sick, and his sisters sent word to Jesus. Here is Jesus' response to the message.

> When Jesus heard that, He said, "This sickness is not unto death, but for the glory of God, that the Son of God may be glorified through it."
>
> John 11:4

Jesus did not leave immediately to go straight to his dear friend's bedside. Instead, he waited two days before going to Bethany, where Lazarus lived. Jesus knew Lazarus was already dead.

> Our friend Lazarus sleeps, but I go that I may wake him up.
>
> John 11:11

By the time Jesus arrived in Bethany, Lazarus had been dead for four days. Now put yourself in the shoes of Martha and Mary. These women knew Jesus personally. They had witnessed and believed in his miraculous power. They had supported his ministry. I would suppose that they had to be at least somewhat aggravated—though they may not have revealed it—at the fact that Jesus allowed their brother to die. Martha makes a statement to Jesus when he arrives. Oh, how I wish we could hear the tone in which this exhausted, grieving woman spoke to her friend and Lord, Jesus.

> Then Martha said to Jesus, "Lord, if You had been here, my brother would not have died. But even now I know that whatever You ask of God, God will give You." Jesus said to her, "Your brother will rise again." Martha said to Him, "I know that he will rise again in the resurrection at the last day."
>
> John 11:21–24

Martha had gone out to meet Jesus. She confessed her belief in him as the Son of God. But this woman is disappointed and broken-hearted, and she surely questioned why Jesus let her brother die.

Mary also gets word that Jesus is near, and she too runs out to meet him, saying the exact same words as Martha: "Lord, if you had been here, my brother would not have died" (see John 11:32).

Maybe your heart burns today with the same thought. You expected Jesus to intervene, and he didn't. You believe in Jesus. You know he has the power to heal. For whatever reason, your prayer has not been answered. Maybe you feel like Jesus has let you down—and you thought you were his friend. Your mind is full of questions that have no answers and well-meaning words from family and friends are no help to you at all. You are not alone.

When Mary made her statement to Jesus, she was on her knees at his feet, weeping. It wouldn't be the only time she wept at his feet. This was the same Mary who would later anoint Jesus' feet with oil and wipe his feet with her hair. But for now, tears of overwhelming grief are flowing from eyes that look to Jesus for hope in her future, for some comfort, for an explanation. It was then that the heart of Jesus broke, not only for these women he loved as dear friends, but also for the grieving people who had followed Mary as she ran to him. Jesus began to groan in the Spirit and weep.

Hurting soul, I want you to pay close attention to three things in this story from John 11. The first thing you must see is that Jesus truly felt the grieving pain of Martha, Mary, and their family and friends. When they hurt, he felt it. This is something you need to grasp. Whatever grief and pain you are going through right now, Jesus is full of compassion and empathy for you.

The next thing to see in this passage is that Jesus did allow Lazarus to die. He always knew what was going on in Bethany. He could have spoke a word from where he was and healed Lazarus or raised him up if he were already dead by the time he got the message. But, according to John 11:4, Jesus chose to wait for the purpose of bringing glory to God. Yes, it was his will *not* to intervene, and Lazarus died. Did God make Lazarus sick? Nothing indicates that he did, but his sovereignty allowed it. Here's the second point: God may not initiate tragedy, but he can use any tragedy.

The third thing to notice is what happened to the group—perhaps a crowd—that followed Mary to Jesus. These people were Jews from Jerusalem. The Jewish leadership in Jerusalem was more than hostile toward Jesus; they had even tried to kill him (see John 11:8). It's likely that some of the crowd with Mary may have been those same Jews, or at least connected to them in some way. Now jump ahead in the story. We all know that Jesus spoke to Lazarus and he walked out of the grave alive. What an exciting result! But perhaps not the best result of the day.

> Then many of the Jews who had come to Mary, and had seen the things Jesus did, believed in Him.
>
> John 11:45

So the third point is that God looks at the big picture and the ultimate good. Jesus wasn't being mean to Martha and Mary by not coming to them sooner. In fact, it broke his heart to see them in such sorrowful agony. But how much more would it break his heart if those same Jews would have died and went to hell if they had not believed in Jesus on that day? Would Martha and Mary want their friends to perish eternally? Of course not! Is that a fair question to ask the grieving soul who has just lost a loved one? Obviously, it never is. But it's comforting to know that when we can't see past the immediate pain of the moment we're in, God always can, he always does, and he always works for the ultimate eternal good. Like he said in Jeremiah, he thinks thoughts of peace and not of evil toward us, and he wants us to have hope in our final outcome. Lazarus, Martha, Mary, and their believing Jewish friends all had a good final outcome in spite of the pain they endured.

We read in the book of James earlier and learned that God cannot tempt us to sin. In a similar vein, when God said in Jeremiah 29:11 that he doesn't think evil or harm toward us, that means he doesn't think thoughts toward us to do us harm. In other words, God doesn't torture us for his own entertainment, and he does not enjoy seeing his people suffer. He certainly does not sit on his throne with a stick waiting to whack whoever steps out of line. There are many avenues that can lead us to pain and suffering. But there is a constant thread throughout the Old and New Testaments of the character of God, and that is he will never think thoughts of evil or harm toward us.

DOES GOD HAVE A HAND IN BRINGING OR ALLOWING SICKNESS?

It's time for the dreaded sticky subject, the one I didn't want to touch with a ten-foot pole. I wanted to just leave this topic out, but too many people are going through trials that involve physical sickness. It just can't be ignored. Does God make us sick? My short answer, straight from my heart, is no. But, as always, we need to see what the Word says and set aside our own thoughts and opinions. I beg you to stick with me until the end of the chapter, for the conclusion may surprise you. Strap your thinkin' caps on and buckle up, kiddos, because this topic isn't easy or for the faint of heart!

Let's begin our quest into this topic in the Old Testament. Miriam, the sister of Moses, was a prophetess, and she led the people in praise and worship. She was obviously anointed and used by the

Lord. But Numbers records how Miriam spoke out against her brother, Moses. Because of her sin of rebellion, Miriam was struck with leprosy—a nasty disease that labeled her unclean according to the Law and required isolation from the general public. God's law required all unclean people to stay outside the camp, so this was also a source of public humiliation for Miriam. However, after seven days, she was allowed back in the camp, which indicated she repented of her sin and was healed.

Miriam's sin—as all sin is—was against God himself, not just her own brother. When Miriam chose to rebel against Moses, she brought judgment upon herself. The text does not say that God himself struck her with leprosy. Did he do it? Did he allow Satan to do it? If a finger were pointed at anyone in this case, it would have to be at Miriam herself. No one escapes the consequences of sin. In some form or fashion, all sin leads to a type of earthly death. We must not overlook the good result in this situation. Miriam repented and God healed her! Once again we see that God doesn't think thoughts of evil or harm toward his people. He wants us to have hope in our final outcome. The final outcome here was that after her time of sickness, isolation, and humiliation, Miriam changed for the better. Could she have prevented the whole episode if she had avoided the temptation to speak out against her brother? I presume so. Would she have been able to overcome the pride and arrogance that caused her to speak out against Moses without this event in her life? Only God knows. Do you suppose she was thankful for the change in her heart's condition? I would like to think so.

Now let's skip ahead to the time when God's people were split into the northern and southern kingdoms of Israel and Judah. A repeating cycle occurred in the history of God's chosen people. They would rebel against God, God would raise up a prophet to warn them of judgment if they did not repent, they ignored the warnings and sometimes even killed the prophets, God would allow an enemy army to persecute the people as his tool of judgment, the people would cry out to God, he would deliver them, and they would serve him for a period of time until the cycle started all over again.

God gave them ample time to break this vicious cycle, but they did not—so harsher judgment eventually came. The northern kingdom of Israel was destroyed by the Assyrians, and the southern kingdom of Judah was carried into captivity by the Babylonians. The Prophet Micah records what God said to his people just prior to the impending judgment. Hold on to your seats for this one!

> Therefore I will also make you sick by striking you, by making you desolate because of your sins…
>
> Micah 6:13

I'm not a Bible scholar, but I can read a dictionary. *Strong's Exhaustive Concordance of the Bible* defines the Hebrew word translated here as *sick* with descriptions of "sick, afflicted, pain, disease, weak, and wounded." This passage doesn't say that God removed a hedge of protection and let the devil do it. God himself says, "I will also make you sick by striking you." I don't know about you, but if anyone is going to hurt me, I prefer it to be someone who loves me and is not set on my ultimate destruction. It is not an evil-thinking God doing this thing. But once again, the finger of responsibility points to the rebellious ones who refused to heed the multiple and patient warnings of God. The good news is that the story does not end with the sickness. Micah prophesied harsh words to God's people, but Micah also fully understood the depth of love and mercy God had for them. He ended his writing with a beautiful description of the character of God.

> Who is a God like You, pardoning iniquity and passing over the transgression of the remnant of His heritage? He does not retain His anger forever, because He delights in mercy. He will again have compassion on us, and will subdue our iniquities. You will cast all our sins into the depths of the sea. You will give truth to Jacob and mercy to Abraham, which You have sworn to our fathers from days of old.
>
> Micah 7:18–20

If God does allow rebellious people to become sick, why would he do it? Not because he's mean, but because he's love. In the case of Miriam, her sickness preceded repentance and restoration. God always wants his rebellious child to turn back to him. Haggai 2 seems to confirm this line of thought, but God used a lack of prosperity instead of sickness. When God's people returned from captivity in Babylon, they were supposed to rebuild the temple, which had been destroyed seventy years earlier by the invading Babylonians. But the returning remnant of God's people soon became indifferent to the temple-rebuilding efforts and instead concentrated on building their own homes. During this time of indifference, the people worked hard, but nothing prospered, including their crops. Crop failure in those days was disastrous. People could literally starve to death. Through the Prophet Haggai, God explained that he was trying to get their attention and cause them to turn back to him.

> "I struck you with blight and mildew and hail in all the labors of your hands; yet you did not turn to Me," says the Lord.
>
> Haggai 2:17

God wanted to prosper them when he brought them home after seventy years in exile. All they had to do was put him first instead of themselves. God didn't strike their crops out of an evil intent, but out of desire to draw them back into the safety of his loving arms.

Now let's explore the New Testament for the same subject. The Corinthian Church had a lot of problems, and Paul wrote a letter to give them clear instruction and good counsel. One of the trouble spots in the church was how they took the Lord's Supper. When they gathered together for the supper, some were in factions, others were gluttonous and didn't leave food for others to eat, and some even went so far as to get drunk during the supper. What a pitiful sight that must have been! It's supposed to be a sacred moment, done in remembrance of the Lord's sacrifice of his body and his blood. Paul addressed these issues and instructed the people to examine themselves so that they would not eat and drink in an unworthy manner.

Now we come to the interesting verse. Some of those who had eaten and drank in an unworthy manner suffered the consequences.

> For he who eats and drinks in an unworthy manner eats and drinks judgment to himself, not discerning the Lord's body. For this reason, many are weak and sick among you, and many sleep.
>
> 1 Corinthians 11:29–30

The selfish and irreverent actions of those who ate and drank in an unworthy manner brought judgment on those individuals. Not eternal judgment—Jesus saved them from that—but God allowed a disciplinary judgment to come upon them in the forms of physical weakness, sickness, and even death. As with the case of Miriam, it doesn't specifically say God put sickness and death on them. It doesn't say Satan did it. Paul says above that they brought the judgment on themselves. All sin brings death to some degree. We will reap what we sow. It's a principle God has set in order, and it applies to every breathing soul on the face of the earth.

We've just seen in the examples of Miriam and the Corinthians that our own sins can bring judgment in the form of sickness in our bodies. Even science today proves this fact. As Christians, we know that un-forgiveness is a sin. Science may call un-forgiveness *bitterness, anger,* or even *stress.* Science has proven that people with bitterness, anger, and stress are prone to sickness and disease. Isn't that a case of a sin bringing judgment on the flesh? We won't go to hell for harboring bitterness, but we'll certainly forfeit the healthy and blessed life that God wanted us to live. We must be careful not to cast blame on God for something that is a result of our own sin.

So now, let's talk about the unexplained sickness. How do we explain why a godly person is struck down by illness or disease? How do we explain why an innocent child is born with a severe handicap? I wish I had a clear-cut answer, but I do not. There are a few things I do know, and past that, all I can say is we'll just have to trust God and be confident in his love for us. Job is an example of unexplained suffering and sickness. So let's look at the life of Job and see what he had to say at the end of all his suffering.

Job was God's champion. God himself said that there was none like him on the earth. God said that Job was blameless and upright, that he feared God and shunned evil. So Job did not open a door and invite this tortuous attack, which included sickness. Satan pointed out that God had put a hedge of protection all around Job and if that hedge were removed, Job would surely curse God to his face. God took Satan up on that challenge and allowed Satan access to Job—so the hedge of protection was removed and Satan gladly commenced his vicious attack. In a single day, Job lost all ten of his children and all his wealth. Read below the amazing way Job responded.

> Then Job arose and tore his robe and shaved his head, and he fell to the ground and worshiped. In all this Job did not sin nor charge God with wrong.
>
> Job 1:20, 22

After Job's terrible losses, God and Satan have a second conversation about Job. God pointed out that Job was still blameless and upright, still feared God, shunned evil, still holding fast to his integrity despite the earthly hell he had just been put through. At that point, Satan told God that if Job were to be sick in his body, he would surely curse God to his face. God allowed Satan to afflict Job physically but ordered him not to take his life. Satan's disease of choice for Job was a condition that produced painful boils throughout his whole body. Even while infectious pus oozed from the sores that covered his body, Job still did not sin against God.

So the question is "Why? What was the point? Why did God allow Satan to torment Job?" I'm not sure an exact answer can be given to that question. But who better to listen to than Job himself to see what he thought about the ordeal? Let's look at the comments Job made about his season of suffering.

> Though He slay me, yet will I trust Him.
>
> Job 13:15

For I know that my Redeemer lives, and He shall stand at last on the earth; and after my skin is destroyed, this I know, that in my flesh I shall see God, whom I shall see for myself, and my eyes shall behold, and not another. How my heart yearns within me!

Job 19:25–27

But He knows the way that I take; when He has tested me, I shall come forth as gold.

Job 23:10

I know that You can do everything, and that no purpose of Yours can be withheld from You.

Job 42:2

I have heard of You by the hearing of the ear, but now my eye sees You.

Job 42:5

Job doesn't give an answer to why, but in the end, that question doesn't seem to be as important to him as the result of the whole trial. Job experienced the worst assaults an evil Satan could dish out. And yet, after enduring such heart breaking grief, economic loss, physical pain, and emotional torment, Job came forth as gold. Job trusted God during his trial, no matter what horrible things happened to him. Through it all, Job came to know and see God in a way he'd never known or seen him before the trial. The relationship Job had with his God was what prevailed. The result of this whole ordeal was that Job had an even more intimate walk with God. That's the testimony! As for you and me, no matter what God in his sovereignty may allow Satan to do to us, we can still trust God. We can come out on the other side of it with a more intimate knowledge of God and a faith that's on its way to perfection.

Today, you may feel as though Satan has unleashed the fury of hell against you. So what do you hold on to? You grab hold of your trust in God and your assurance of his love for you. You hold on to your relationship with God and your confidence in his sovereignty.

You hold on to the fact that God doesn't think thoughts of evil or harm toward you. You hold on to a God who's concerned about your final outcome. In the end, sweet one, you will come forth as gold. You will know him in a more intimate way. You will have endured by his grace.

Paul spoke of having a "thorn in his flesh" (see 2 Corinthians 12:7). Bible scholars debate whether it was a physical condition or a demonic spirit. Paul believed in the healing power of Christ. Paul also understood the authority Jesus transferred to his believers in regard to demonic spirits. In no way are we talking about a man who was ignorant of the provisions of God or ignorant on how to battle Satan in the spiritual realm. In fact, in 2 Corinthians 12—before Paul speaks of this thorn in his flesh—he talks about being caught up to the third heaven and hearing words that weren't lawful for him to speak. Whatever this thorn in Paul's flesh was, we know it came from Satan. Paul pleaded with God three times for deliverance, and God basically said no. In the absence of a deliverance from whatever this affliction or aggravation was, read how Paul felt about it.

> And lest I should be exalted above measure by the abundance of the revelations, a thorn in the flesh was given to me, a messenger of Satan to buffet me, lest I be exalted above measure. Concerning this thing I pleaded with the Lord three times that it might depart from me. And He said to me, "My grace is sufficient for you, for My strength is made perfect in weakness." Therefore most gladly I will rather boast in my infirmities, that the power of Christ may rest upon me. Therefore I take pleasure in infirmities, in reproaches, in needs, in persecutions, in distresses, for Christ's sake. For when I am weak, then I am strong.
>
> 2 Corinthians 12:7–10

Paul doesn't use the word *thankful*, but it sounds as if he is thankful when he says he takes pleasure in infirmities, reproaches, needs, persecutions, and distresses. Of course, no rational human would choose such things. But if the sovereign hand of God allows these types of things in the lives of his own, they should embrace whatever brings glory to God. Above all else, Paul knew he could trust God to allow whatever it took to give Paul a good final outcome. God allowed Satan to aggravate Paul with this thorn, and at the same time God gave Paul the grace to not only endure it, but to embrace it! That's the point I prefer to focus on—that God's grace is sufficient for whatever we face. When you and I plead with God for something and don't get the answer we seek, we can be assured that he will give us grace and it will be sufficient.

We've seen that individuals can sin and bring a judgment of sickness on themselves. We've also seen that God will sometimes allow Satan to attack us with physical sickness or aggravation. We also live in a fallen world, and sickness will sometimes simply be a part of living in it. But one thing we do not see in the New Testament—as opposed to the Old Testament—is God clearly stating that he strikes anyone, causing them to be sick. Does God allow physical pain? Obviously, yes, or else he's not sovereign. Does he use that pain for a greater purpose? I believe he does. There isn't anything so bad that God cannot use it for good. Does he use sickness in judgment during this time of the new covenant and grace? Not that I know of. (Note: God will pour out his wrath on unbelievers in the book of Revelation, and sickness will be part of that judgment.) But there is one New Testament event that we must consider. Acts 5 tells of Ananias and Sapphira, husband and wife, who were believers that lied to the Holy Spirit. They were not struck with sickness but rather, were immediately struck dead. That's obviously a judgment on their sin. Does it still happen today? I don't know, but I wouldn't risk lying to the Holy Spirit!

When we are sick God can certainly use that sickness to teach us or give us insight into something. Years ago I woke suddenly in the middle of the night with a pain that was almost more than I could bear. The doctors in our local emergency room eventually determined that it was a kidney stone, and I was given morphine for the pain. I believe my own poor dietary choices were to blame for causing the kidney stone to form. But God used that experience to teach me to have more compassion for people in pain. I have a fairly high tolerance for pain, and before I had a kidney stone, I thought people in pain should just toughen up when they were hurting. God used my physical pain to teach me to have more compassion for people in pain. Did God give me a kidney stone? I don't believe so. Am I thankful for what I learned in the pain of passing a kidney stone? I absolutely am.

Please understand that I absolutely believe in the healing power of God. I believe that Jesus bore our sickness and pain on the cross and that by his stripes we were healed. But the sad and undeniable fact is people don't always get healed when we pray, and I simply cannot explain that. Some want to point fingers and accuse people of a lack of faith. That may be the situation in some cases, but I dare say not in all of them. I think we need to be very careful with blanket statements on such a complicated topic as healing. I also think we ought to avoid arguments trying to defend God's integrity on this issue. He's big enough to defend himself, and some situations are just beyond our human comprehension.

I heard a story of a young soldier fighting in the jungles of Vietnam who was injured and sent to the MASH unit. While he lay in the hospital, two of his buddies were killed by an explosion while in their foxhole. Had he not been injured, he likely would have died along with them. Was the injury allowed by God to spare his life? I don't know, but I'm so very thankful he was hurt, because that man was my uncle. Years later, he was instrumental in the salvations and spiritual growth of our family.

How can we explain some of the stories told after the 9/11 tragedy? Some employees who worked at the World Trade Center were sick that particular day and were spared from certain death. Was it a coincidence? Did God allow it to spare the lives of those he had a purpose for? What mortal can possibly answer these questions, and is it even fruitful to try? I am certain in God's love and care for me, and I trust whatever his sovereignty will allow in my life. How could I not trust the one who numbers every hair on my head?

Are not two sparrows sold for a copper coin? And not one of them falls to the ground apart from your Father's will. But the very hairs of your head are all numbered. Do not fear therefore; you are of more value than many sparrows.

Matthew 10:29–31

I don't think we can wrap our finite human minds around all the things of God. When we are puzzled about trials and struggling to understand, we can apply the following passages to our troubled hearts.

Trust in the Lord with all your heart, and lean not on your own understanding...

Proverbs 3:5

Oh, the depth of the riches both of the wisdom and knowledge of God! How unsearchable are His judgments and His ways past finding out!

Romans 11:33

People often argue that it is the thief—referring to Satan—that comes to steal, kill, and destroy and that Jesus has come to give us abundant life. That's absolutely true. However, the book of James says that the Lawgiver—referring to Jesus—is able to save and destroy. Let's look at both verses.

The thief does not come except to steal, and to kill, and to destroy. I have come that they may have life, and that they may have it more abundantly.

John 10:10

There is one Lawgiver, who is able to save and to destroy. Who are you to judge another?

James 4:12

Let's focus in on the word *destroy* used in both passages. Both words come from the same Greek word that means to utterly destroy. So both Jesus and Satan are capable of destroying. But—pay close attention here and don't misunderstand—Jesus is not capable of sin. His motives will always be pure. Satan's motives are always evil. If the hand of Jesus is ever involved in any type of destruction, there will be a pure motive behind it, and it will never be to harm his own people, but only to do them an ultimate good. The book of James explains this even further.

> My brethren, take the prophets, who spoke in the name of the Lord, as an example of suffering and patience. Indeed we count them blessed who endure. You have heard of the perseverance of Job and seen the end intended by the Lord—that the Lord is very compassionate and merciful.
>
> James 5:10–11

We can trust the compassionate and merciful Jesus. Able to destroy, yes, but if he does, he has a purpose in the end intended. I see it in this plain and simple example. Suppose my home had a dangerous mold growing behind the walls, and I had no idea it was there. That mold would be destroying my family and me and—left alone—could spread and cause us great health problems. But if I turned my home over to a mold expert, he could detect the danger I could not see and begin to remediate the mold. The mold expert would destroy the moldy sheetrock and remove it from my home. It would be an aggravating mess and very costly. But the end result would be for my ultimate good. Only God can look behind the walls of our hearts and see what evils lurk there with an intention to destroy us. Because he loves us and intends good for us, he may allow some destroying to purge out of us what needs purged. And only God can see ahead to the end intended and know what is for our own good. We just have to trust him.

Let's recap. God doesn't think evil or harm to you. Your own sin may bring judgment upon you in some form—including sickness. God sometimes allows Satan access to you, but God will always work things out for a good final outcome for you and give you sufficient grace for each day. Sometimes you just can't make sense of your trials, but you can still trust the Lord and respond to your trials by running into his loving embrace.

> As a father pities his children, so the Lord pities those who fear Him. For He knows our frame; He remembers that we are dust.
>
> Psalm 103:13–14

"Daddy, please don't let them put anymore ice on me." These were the words my youngest sister, Kim, said to our daddy as she lay shaking in a hospital bed in Collinsville, Oklahoma. Her frail little body was burning with a high fever as it tried to fight the pneumonia in her tiny lungs. She was just four years old, and Daddy struggled not to cry as she begged him to stop the nurses from icing her down. She was his baby, and he would have taken her place if it were possible. He couldn't stand seeing her shivering in that bed, but he knew what had to be done to save her life. He sat by her bed, watching her every move and having pity on her, just like the verse above says. Except his pity was not the kind of pity we think of in our English language today.

We can have pity on the homeless man in a back alley, but not really love him. In Psalm 103, the word *pity* means "to love deeply, with compassion and mercy." That's how Daddy felt about his little Kimberly Ann. That's how our Abba Father—our heavenly Daddy—feels about you and me when we're sick and suffering. Nothing that happens to us misses his watchful gaze. If we're suffering, he's hurting with us, but he won't stop something that is for our own good, even if we beg him to. Daddy cringed with every bag of ice placed around Kim's fevered body, but he let the nurses do what was necessary because of his great pity—love, compassion and mercy—for her. Oh, suffering saint, your heavenly Daddy has pity on you also. Kim survived pneumonia in the winter of 1969, and through it all, God was glorified as we thanked him for sparing her life.

I do want to make clear that sometimes illness is oppression of the devil, straight from the evil pits of hell. In those cases, we should resist the devil, exercise our faith, and seek healing for the oppressed.

> How God anointed Jesus of Nazareth with the Holy Spirit and with power, who went about doing good and healing all who were oppressed by the devil, for God was with Him.
>
> Acts 10:38

> When evening had come, they brought to him many who were demon-possessed. And He cast out the spirits with a word, and healed all who were sick, that it might be fulfilled which was spoken by Isaiah the prophet, saying: "He Himself took our infirmities and bore our sicknesses."
>
> Matthew 8:16–17

These verses clearly indicate that some sicknesses are from demonic oppression. These sicknesses should be a call to battle for the Christian. We should run confidently to the battle when the Holy Spirit leads and use the name of Jesus and the authority he has given us to fight our evil enemy and claim the healing Jesus made available to us on the cross.

Other times, there are infirmities that we just cannot explain. There are diseases and conditions that have no obvious explanation to the believer, and in our human condition, we cannot make sense of the tragedies of them. In those cases, we can look to the Gospel of John, which records an interesting story about a man born blind.

When the disciples saw this man, they asked Jesus who had sinned to cause the man to be born blind—his parents or himself. Get a grasp on what their belief was. They believed sin caused blindness, and they also believed that an unborn child was capable of sin. Read the response of Jesus.

> Jesus answered, "Neither this man nor his parents sinned, but that the works of God should be revealed in him."
>
> John 9:3

Jesus blamed no one for the blinded man's condition. The blindness was allowed so that glory could be brought to God. Jesus healed the man's eyes, God was glorified, and the formerly blinded man also had his spiritual eyes opened to believe in Jesus as the Messiah.

Life is filled with many trials, problems, sufferings, and pain; and we always want to know *why*. Sometimes we'll know, sometimes we'll never know. But in the end, is knowing really all that important? Does it really matter why a trial comes, as long as we keep walking with God and he gets all the glory? Read below what Jesus prayed.

> Now My soul is troubled, and what shall I say? "Father, save Me from this hour"? But for this purpose I came to this hour. "Father, glorify Your name."
>
> John 12:27–28

Jesus came to earth to die on the cross, redeem the world, and reconcile fallen man to his Father. He admitted that he was troubled about what he was about to endure, but look at his prayer in the midst of his dread: "Father, glorify your name." What an example for us! When we face trials, shouldn't this also be our prayer? We may be hurting beyond what we think we can bear, but in the midst of it, we can still pray, "Father, glorify your name!" His glory takes precedence over our pain—or our need to know.

I doubt that we'll ever fully understand all this until we get to the other side. I do believe in applying to my life the old saying "whatever doesn't kill me will only make me stronger!" I also believe that every Christian has a choice to make when faced with a trial. We can choose to lean on God, seek him, and come out victorious; or we can cower down and let Satan beat us up in our trial. I encourage you to fight with the whole armor of God and trust God no matter what he allows to come your way, remembering that he does not think thoughts of evil or harm toward you. Whatever you face, there's always grace, grace, marvelous grace, and it's always sufficient for your needs. So when you feel the urge to ask "Why me, Lord?" won't you consider saying instead, "Father, glorify your name."

IS YOUR PATH GOOD OR BAD?

The TV show *Hee Haw* was one of the longest-running shows in television history. My parents were huge fans, and our family rarely missed an episode. I'm reminded of a recurring skit from the show with Archie Campbell, the barber, telling Roy Clark about his misfortune.

"Did you hear that my great-uncle died?"

"Oh, that's bad," replies Roy.

"No, that's good," says Archie. "He left me $50,000!"

"Oh, that's good!"

"No, that's bad. By the time the IRS got finished, I only had $25,000."

"Oh, that is bad!"

"No, that's good, I bought me an airplane!"

"Oh, that is good!"

"No, that's bad. I learned to fly it, and I fell out of it!"

The skit continues back and forth until Archie reports that his wife left him and both men agreed that was good! This comedy sketch reminds me that often what may look bad in our eyes may look good in God's eyes.

When man fell in the garden of Eden, there were consequences for it. Adam's rebellion against God brought a curse upon mankind and the earth. That same rebellion also cost Adam and Eve the luxury of living in the paradise God had prepared for them. The couple was banished from the garden and sent out to till the cursed ground. Can you imagine what their eyes must have beheld as they left the beautiful garden of Eden? I imagine them stepping out of a sanctuary of brilliant colors, aromatic fragrances, dappled shade, and gentle breezes into a burning hot, dry and dusty ground—a barren wilderness. That night they would not lay their heads on a soft bed of green grass, but likely on hard, rocky ground surrounded by thorns and thistles. It looks like a sad day, with Adam and Eve being punished by a Holy God. But is that what it really was?

> Then the Lord God said, "Behold, the man has become like one of Us, to know good and evil. And now, lest he put out his hand and take also of the tree of life, and eat, and live forever"—therefore the Lord God sent him out of the garden of Eden to till the ground from which he was taken. So He drove out the man; and He placed cherubim at the east of the garden of Eden, and a flaming sword which turned every way, to guard the way to the tree of life.
>
> Genesis 3:22–24

What may have looked bad from a human perspective was actually good. It was God's love and mercy for man that drove Adam and Eve out of the garden. Besides the tree of knowledge of good and evil, there was also a tree of life in that garden. If Adam and Eve had eaten of the tree of life after they had sinned, they would have lived forever in their sinful condition. God loved them too much to let that happen, so he drove them out of the garden and placed a cherubim and a flaming sword around the tree of life so no man could ever eat of it until safely in the presence of God (Revelation 2:7). What Adam and Eve may have viewed as punishment was actually the grace and mercy of their loving heavenly Father. It was God providing for their future reconciliation with him through his Son, who was slain before the foundation of the world (Revelation 13:8)! Oh, give thanks to God for his great love and trust him in the situations that you think are bad for you!

Some people just refuse to believe that God's plan for us could ever include anything painful or difficult. In the beginning, before the fall of man, that was probably the case. God's original plan was perfect communion between Creator and creation. That was the situation before man sinned in rebellion against his Creator. God still wants ultimate good for us, but with sin being a factor in the world we live, it's a brand-new ballgame. We can't always explain it, understand it, or even like it from this side of heaven, but the fact remains: God's plans for us now may include rocky paths. How else can we explain the story of the Prophet Hosea, whom God instructed to marry a prostitute and raise children who weren't his own? Surely that plan caused Hosea to suffer great heartache. What about Paul, who suffered brutal persecutions as he took the gospel across his world? The sufferings of Paul are almost beyond belief. He lists some of them in 2 Corinthians 11. I dare any of us to endure one of these, let alone them all! Paul was imprisoned often, beaten by Jewish authorities five times, beaten with rods three times, stoned once, shipwrecked three times, spent a night and a day in the ocean, faced robbers, hurt by his own people and foreigners, been sleep deprived, hungry, thirsty, cold, and naked. Yet we never read that Paul was out of God's will or that he had a lack of faith. So we must conclude that these events played into God's sovereign plan as Paul took the gospel to the Gentiles. Yes, Paul suffered, but compared to the souls he won for Christ, he took pleasure in the things he had suffered for Christ's sake (2 Corinthians 12:10). On the surface, Paul's path looked bad, but from the viewpoint of heaven, what a good and glorious path it was! We tend to focus on the natural, but the eternal—and God's purposes—are what really matter.

For our light affliction, which is but for a moment, is working for us a far more exceeding and eternal weight of glory, while we do not look at the things which are seen, but at the things which are not seen. For the things which are seen are temporary, but the things which are not seen are eternal.

2 Corinthians 4:17–18

With the benefit of 20/20 hindsight, we can see the big picture and give thanks to God for how he used both Hosea and Paul. But I wonder about the emotions of those two men in the midst of their trials. They were made of human flesh like you and I are. I'm sure they had moments of struggle, just like you and I do today. We're told that the Bible is written partly as an example for us. We can look at the difficult, sacrificial paths of both Hosea and Paul, and see the good that came from both. In Hosea's case, God's people had insight into his unconditional love for them. In Paul's case, no one else had the impact on the establishment of the early church as he did, and he wrote more of the New Testament than anyone else. Both men obeyed God at great costs to themselves. Their paths were brutally difficult in the natural, but the eternal payoff proved that the paths were in all reality good—because God is always good.

Being a woman and a mother, I love the story of Hannah. She was a woman who also walked a path that looked bad to the natural eye. She was barren in a time when childless married women were thought to be under the judgment of God. Her heartfelt longing for a child was complicated by the condemning eyes of her peers and the distress of living with her husband's other wife. Peninnah was Hannah's rival. Hannah had her husband Elkanah's heart, but Peninnah had his children, along with a spiteful attitude set on hurting Hannah at every opportunity.

And whenever the time came for Elkanah to make an offering, he would give portions to Peninnah his wife and to all her sons and daughters. But to Hannah he would give a double portion, for he loved Hannah although the Lord had closed her womb. And her rival also provoked her severely, to make her miserable, because the Lord had closed her womb.

1 Samuel 1:4–6

Hannah walked a difficult path—bad from a natural viewpoint. But reading the verse above shows us that our sovereign God was always in control. Notice that twice in the passage it is made very clear that the Lord had closed her womb. Hannah's path was one of feeling abandoned by her God and persecuted by her enemy. Let's see where this dreadful path takes her.

> And she was in bitterness of soul, and prayed to the Lord and wept in anguish. Then she made a vow and said, "O Lord of hosts, if You will indeed look on the affliction of your maidservant and remember me, and not forget your maidservant, but will give your maidservant a male child, then I will give him to the Lord all the days of his life."
>
> 1 Samuel 1:10–11

Hannah's path brought her to her knees in prayer, seeking the Lord. Of course she wanted a son, but I think her true heart's desire was having the approval of God in her life. A son would be a sign to her of that approval. The rest of the story is an answered prayer. God indeed blessed Hannah with a son, and more children soon followed. She kept her vow and gave Samuel to God, who used him as a prophet and judge among God's people.

I heard Rod Parsley say in a televised sermon a statement that I found fascinating: "A friend rejoices where you are . . . an enemy pushes you to where you are supposed to be!" Look at your trial and see where it's pushing you. Is it pushing you to your knees? Is it pushing you into a more intimate knowledge of your heavenly Father? Is it pushing you to prioritize your life? Is it pushing you to stop taking your loved ones for granted? Is it pushing you to evaluate your spiritual walk, and purge some un-Christlike attitudes from your soul? Is it pushing you to follow the will of God for your life and quit trying to control what paths you walk? If you would just take your eyes off yourself, you just might see where you are really going! With a sovereign God in control, even your enemy can be used to keep your feet on a path that is good!

Perhaps the most skewed perspective of good versus bad is the crucifixion of Christ. Many people view it as a tragedy. No doubt it was the cruelest and most agonizing event that human or divine eyes would ever witness. But it was not a tragedy. It was a victory!

Yet it pleased the Lord to bruise Him.

Isaiah 53:10

One amazing reality of the crucifixion is that David prophetically foretold the exact details of it in Psalm 22. Not only were the physical details mentioned, like casting lots for Jesus' clothes and the brutal way he was beaten and pierced, but even the emotions Jesus felt were listed. In fact, Psalm 22 begins with the emotion of feeling forsaken.

My God, My God, why have You forsaken Me? Why are You so far from helping Me, and from the words of My groaning?

Psalm 22:1

Continuing to look at the prophetic Psalm 22, let's remember that the entire psalm deals with the crucifixion, and read what the Father God was doing while his Son hung on the cross.

You have answered Me.

Psalm 22:21

For He has not despised nor abhorred the affliction of the afflicted; nor has He hidden His face from Him; but when He cried to Him, He heard.

Psalm 22:24

God was there, he heard, and he answered! Jesus felt forsaken, and for a moment, he bore the weight of our sin all alone, but God was there. He heard every cry from the cross, and he answered. Was it a painful path? Most definitely it was. Was it a good path? It surely was. The end intended was salvation for us and glory for God!

Consider the missionary team of men in the 1950s who willingly laid down their lives to bring the gospel to the dangerous Waodoni tribe in the jungle of Ecuador. Their inspiring story is recorded in the book *Through Gates of Splendor* and the movie *End of the Spear.* These men purposed not to defend themselves, which they were quite capable of doing, so they could reach these lost souls. The Holy Spirit empowered them to accomplish their mission, and today the Waodoni tribe is predominantly Christian. Yes, the Holy Spirit is sent to give us power, but the ultimate goal of that power is to win souls for Jesus. Perhaps someone is watching your current trial, closely examining your reaction to it, observing the grace and strength God supplies you every day, and you may be the very tool God uses to bring them into the fold. Isn't that a good path and something to be thankful for?

Hurting heart, please grasp this concept. In the middle of your trial, see the whole path, looking both at where you've been and at where you are going. Try not to focus only on the present moment when you feel hurt, tired, abandoned, or unloved. God is there, precious one, and he hears you and he answers you! Your result will be victory—however God may define that—and he will be glorified as you walk this path.

A final example of a difficult path is the story of the early church. Before Jesus ascended to heaven, he promised to send the Holy Spirit to his believers. Read below how Jesus also prophesied of a difficult path the early church would take.

> But you shall receive power when the Holy Spirit has come upon you; and you shall be witnesses to Me in Jerusalem, and in all Judea and Samaria, and to the end of the earth.
>
> Acts 1:8

History records that every time persecution comes to the church, the church experiences tremendous growth. In Acts 1:8, Jesus promises to send the Holy Spirit, who will give them power. Oh, how we love the idea of having power! But the rest of the verse says we will be witnesses in Jerusalem, Judea, and Samaria and to the ends of the earth. It's the Holy Spirit that provided the early Christians the power to endure the severe persecutions that drove them out of Jerusalem—to the ends of the earth—thereby spreading the gospel of Christ. Had life been pleasant and grand in Jerusalem for those early believers, the gospel may have never left the country. But their bad path, which made them flee Jerusalem for the sake of their very lives, took the gospel all over the world. What a good path!

It is easier to go down a hill than up, but the view is from the top!

—Arnold Bennett

PART TWO:
MY TRIALS AND WHY I'M THANKFUL FOR THEM

THE SCIENCE OF GRATITUDE

Gratitude is the heart's memory.

French Proverb

The Word of God contains all the instructions on thanksgiving and gratitude for us Christians to study, learn, and apply to our lives. Yet seldom do we fully grasp and implement the concepts of gratitude into our daily prayers and the thoughts we think—our thought lives. The New Age world, on the other hand, has not only grasped this concept, but they've acted upon it and improved their lives. How sad that we've neglected such a wonderful treasure in the Bible by not guarding our thought lives and being more thankful. It has caused us to fall short of our heavenly Father's expectations and not reap the benefits he intended for us to enjoy.

I have come across some interesting information that I believe confirms what the Bible teaches about the impact of proper thinking, especially in regard to thoughts of gratitude. Let me preface it all by pointing out that I am only relaying information I've read. The information makes perfect sense to me and in my opinion, completely lines up with the Holy Scriptures. However, some of the sources of this information are not entirely Christian, and I hesitate to point anyone in the direction of those sources. So if you find this chapter fascinating and if you do further research on your own, I beg you to do so with great discernment and reject anything that does not line up with the Bible or that claims any other source of power except Jesus Christ alone and his Lordship.

Science has proven that all matter in our universe moves because it possesses energy. Under a high-powered microscope, motion can be seen in an object that appears to be still because molecules move. In medicine we see the measurement of electrical energy in the body. The brain is electric, and an EEG reads that electrical energy. An ECG traces the electrical changes in the heart. We may not see the energy with our naked eyes, but we know it's there, just as we know that radio waves exist, even though they cannot be seen either. The energy everything contains can be measured by its frequency. Even our thoughts and emotions produce energy that many sources claim can be measured by their frequencies. These sources claim that the better emotions and thoughts—like love and gratitude—measure a higher frequency than other emotions like anger and fear, which measure much lower frequencies. In fact, from what I've read on this topic in various books and Web sites, the emotional thought that is often claimed to carry one of the highest—if not *the* highest—frequencies is gratitude.

This may sound a bit farfetched to some readers, so let me give you a few examples to help explain. A cartoon example of this energy concept would be the characters of Tigger and Eyeore from *Winnie the Pooh*. Tigger is happy, optimistic, and bounces everywhere he goes; he is full of high energy. In contrast, Eyeore is depressed, pessimistic, and moves as slow as molasses; he has a low energy vibration. The opposite thought lives of both characters reflect their opposite energy levels and expressions—the vibes they put out.

We've all experienced feeling the emotions that a person projects, the vibes he or she sends out. Surely all of us have had a strange feeling and looked over our shoulder to find someone staring at us. How can we explain that feeling if there wasn't an energy being sent our direction? A friend of mine recently walked into her business at night and immediately felt someone was in there with an evil intent.

She was right; she had walked in on a robbery! In her case, she correctly attributed that feeling to the Holy Spirit and called on Jesus for protection. Thankfully, the robbers were frightened away and she was unharmed. But even non-Christians have had similar experiences to these examples because we all have and feel energy.

While some readers may still question how our thoughts and emotions could be measured in a type of electromagnetic frequency, marketing professionals already use various techniques to measure the emotional reactions of potential customers to their advertisements. Some claim that even the energy of a color can be measured. I really don't know about that, but I do know that a lot of research money has been spent on color and its effect on humans. Have you ever noticed how many restaurants are decorated in red? We're told that the color red stimulates our appetites. How could a color stimulate us unless it contained energy? Do you notice that some colors just make you feel good? They likely contain higher frequencies of energy. We can even go so far as to say that certain colors make some of us feel good and the rest of us not so good. Perhaps it has to do with our differing skin tones. People with cooler skin tones feel better in cool-toned clothes because it complements their skin tone. Couldn't a complementing magnetic energy between the skin and color of the clothes explain this? Every woman knows what clothes in her wardrobe make her look good and feel good. It must be energy!

Along the same line, think about the people in your life who make you feel good whenever you are around them. You'll notice that they tend to be optimistic, encouraging, and most likely grateful for what they have. On the contrary, you also have people in your life that tend to depress you emotionally when you are around them. They are more apt to be pessimistic people who are depressed, complaining, angry, or ungrateful. The differences in the emotions and thought lives of people explain why you do or don't enjoy their company. You have people in your life who lift you up and others who drag you down simply by being in their presence—around their energy.

How can you feel what they are feeling if there isn't energy in those emotions? When you walk into a funeral home to visit a grieving family, the energy in the room is heavy; it has a low frequency, and you can feel it. When you get a phone call from an excited friend who has good news to share, you can feel the emotion over the phone line. You don't even have to physically be in their presence to feel the energy of their happiness.

I found a study by Robert A. Emmons (University of California, Davis) and Michael E. McCullough (University of Miami) titled "Counting Blessings Versus Burdens: An Experimental Investigation of Gratitude and Subjective Well-Being in Daily Life." Below is the opening paragraph of their research.

> The effect of a grateful outlook on psychological and physical well-being was examined. In Studies 1 and 2, participants were randomly assigned to 1 of 3 experimental conditions (hassles, gratitude listing, and either neutral life events or social comparison); they then kept weekly (Study 1) or daily (Study 2) records of their moods, coping behaviors, health behaviors, physical symptoms, and overall life appraisals. In a 3rd study, persons with neuromuscular disease were randomly assigned to either the gratitude condition or to a control condition. The gratitude-outlook groups exhibited heightened well-being across several, though not all, of the outcome measures across the 3 studies, relative to the comparison groups. The effect on positive affect appeared to be the most robust finding. Results suggest that a conscious focus on blessings may have emotional and interpersonal benefits.

Don't you just love it when scientific research confirms what the Bible said thousands of years ago? No wonder the Bible tells us to give thanks in everything! It has emotional and interpersonal benefits, according to the scientific data.

> For as he thinks in his heart, so is he.
>
> Proverbs 23:7

I wish I understood the Hebrew language so I could fully understand the word translated above as *thinks. Strong's Exhaustive Concordance of the Bible* defines it as "to split or open, to act as gate-keeper, to estimate; think." The word *gatekeeper* grabs my attention. I picture a mini-version of myself standing at the gate of my brain, determining which thoughts can come in and which thoughts must get out. Whatever my gatekeeper allows to take up residence in my brain will determine who I am. How can we not comprehend something so simple? If we truly understood the simple "think good, feel good" instruction, we wouldn't be spending billions of dollars on feel-good medications. (Note: I understand that medication is necessary in many cases, so please don't think I'm unsympathetic to those on anti-depressant medications. However, it's generally believed that these medications are overly prescribed in our population, and that's what I'm referring to in this point. I would not purposely offend anyone on this issue.) My point is that we should follow God's prescription for good mental health—think right!

There is fascinating Japanese research by Dr. Emoto on the effect of ideas, words, and music upon the molecules of water. He compares water from clear mountain streams to water from polluted or stagnant sources. The water from the pristine waters formed beautiful crystalline structures—which look like intricately designed and symmetrical snowflakes—as opposed to the polluted water, which formed ugly and deformed structures. In further research by Dr. Emoto, the words *thank you* were taped to a bottle of distilled water. Frozen crystals from that water had a similar shape to crystals formed by water that had been exposed to music from Bach's "Goldberg Variations," which is music composed out of gratitude to the man it was named for. Isn't that interesting? It proves that our world was designed by a Creator who didn't overlook even the tiniest details of his creation when he caused water exposed to the energy of gratitude to produce similar frozen crystal patterns. And should it surprise us that our world responds to words? After all, it was created by the powerful spoken Word of God! Amazing!

Dr. Emoto was asked if he had found a particular word or phrase in his research that he found to be most helpful in cleaning up the natural waters of the world. Here is a portion of his reply:

Yes. There is a special combination that seems to be perfect for this, which is love plus the combination of thanks and appreciation reflected in the English word *gratitude.* Just one of these is not enough. Love needs to be based in gratitude, and gratitude needs to be based in love. These two words together create the most important vibration.

In my opinion, this research underscores what the Word of God has said for thousands of years. Our thoughts and attitudes determine what we feel and what we become. It's up to each one of us to be good gatekeepers of our minds, determining what is acceptable to take up residence there. A good gatekeeper—a good thinker—will transform him or herself.

> And do not be conformed to this world, but be transformed by the renewing of your mind.
>
> Romans 12:2

The Camelot Inn in Tulsa, Oklahoma, was a distinguished and recognizable hotel for those of us in Oklahoma's Green Country. It resembled a castle, and as a young adult, I was excited to see it in the movie *Tex.* But since its charming beginnings decades ago, the Camelot Inn fell into disrepair. Gone were the paying guests, including a former president of the United States, who used to stay in its lovely rooms. They were eventually replaced by transients, and the building was damaged beyond repair, so the once-famous Camelot Inn was condemned and torn down.

I share the story of the Camelot Inn so it can be compared to our minds. Our minds were made by God, and his design was for us to keep thankfulness at the forefront. When we refuse—or are too neglectful—to have a thankful mind, there is an empty space, and nature demands that vacuums be filled with something. When thankful thoughts are not in our minds, then what kinds of thoughts are in our minds? I think it's just like the Camelot Inn story. When the nice guests stopped coming to the Camelot Inn, it created a vacuum at the old hotel, and they were eventually replaced by people whose lifestyles led to the ultimate destruction of the historic hotel. If we don't keep thankful thoughts in our minds, they will soon fill with thoughts and mindsets that lead to our ultimate destruction. I'm not referring to eternal destruction, but at the very least, earthly damage will be done when our minds are void of thanksgiving. Paul gave an admonition to the Christians at Ephesus that reinforces this idea. In the following verse, Paul is referring to obscenity and dirty jokes that can fill the minds of those who fail to keep thankfulness a priority in their thought process.

> Nor should there be obscenity, foolish talk or coarse joking, which are out of place, but rather thanksgiving.
>
> Ephesians 5:4 (NIV)

If we would only concentrate on thanksgiving and gratitude, there would be no room left over for selfish, hateful, or obscene thoughts in our minds. Our society is quickly losing the concept of gratitude. We're quick to blame others, we're not thankful for what we have, and we carry a chip on our shoulders, resenting someone who has more than we do. There tends to be a consensus in America today that we are owed something. When did that attitude creep up on us? We need to clean up our cluttered minds and be a grateful nation—grateful for the air we breathe; for our food, shelter, and clothing; for a free nation; for the soldiers who defend our freedom; for the loved ones in our lives; and for a loving God who extends his merciful hand to us with the offer of salvation.

> Gratitude is not only the greatest of virtues, but the parent of all others.
>
> —Cicero

Isn't it so backward that some of the first words parents teach children are "thank you," yet grateful hearts seem to be few and far between? This isn't a new phenomenon. Let's visit the story of the ten lepers that Jesus healed as recorded in Luke 17. When Jesus passed through a certain village, he encountered ten lepers yelling out to him for mercy. They would have been yelling because they were afar off. The law demanded that lepers keep a safe distance away from people because of their contagious disease. So we must understand the isolation these men lived in. They were doomed to lonely and painful lives in their physical condition, relying on the pity and compassion of others for their very sustenance. Besides all that, the leprosy was a nasty skin condition that they had to take care of without our modern conveniences of medication—or even running water! These men had nothing to lose in yelling out to Jesus and begging for mercy. Without making a big production of healing these men, Jesus simply told them to go show themselves to the priests. The law required an unclean person to be declared clean by a priest before reentering society. As the men went to the priests, they were healed of this dreaded disease. Ten miserable, suffering, lonely, and destitute men were healed. But were they grateful?

> Now one of them, when he saw that he was healed, returned, and with a loud voice glorified God, and fell down on his face at His feet, giving Him thanks. And he was a Samaritan. So Jesus answered and said, "Were there not ten cleansed? But where are the nine? Were there not any found who returned to give glory to God except this foreigner?" And He said to him, "Arise, go your way. Your faith has made you well."
>
> Luke 17:15–19

All ten men were physically healed. But Jesus made a statement to the grateful man that indicates he alone received a spiritual healing—eternal salvation. The *NIV Study Bible* commentary states that the phrase "your faith has made you well" may be rendered "your faith has saved you." The man's thankful heart led to a faith that saved his soul. The *Wycliffe Bible Commentary* states on the same subject that "gratitude was even rarer than faith." Isn't that the truth? Today we see people quick to receive healing or help from the Lord, but not so quick to go back and say thank you with a heart so full of gratitude that it changes their very spiritual condition. The thankful man remembered what he had been delivered of, and he was grateful. Oh, that more Christians today would remember how they've been snatched away from eternal torment in hell and healed of their diseases—and be grateful.

> Bless the Lord, O my soul, and forget not all His benefits: Who forgives all your iniquities, Who heals all your diseases, Who redeems your life from destruction, Who crowns you with lovingkindness and tender mercies, Who satisfies your mouth with good things so that your youth is renewed like the eagle's.
>
> Psalm 103:2–5

We should not forget all his benefits. When we remember all the Lord has done for us, our minds should fill with so much gratitude that nothing else has room to take up residence there. And when we think on those things, it produces energy—"your youth is renewed like the eagle's." When we remember the Lord's benefits to us with a grateful heart, then we experience youthful and powerful energy. What a deal! But wait, there's more.

> Be anxious for nothing, but in everything by prayer and supplication, with thanksgiving, let your requests be made known to God; and the peace of God, which surpasses all understanding, will guard your hearts and minds through Christ Jesus. Finally, brethren, whatever things are true, whatever things are noble, whatever things are just, whatever things are pure, whatever things are lovely, whatever things are of good report, if there is any virtue and if there is anything praiseworthy—meditate on these things. The things which you learned and received and heard and saw in me, these do, and the God of peace will be with you.
>
> Philippians 4:6–9

We find another promise in the above passage for having a thankful mind. When we pray with thanksgiving, God gives us peace. Not just any kind of peace, but a peace that will guard—as if it were a gatekeeper—our hearts and minds. Then the passage continues to give us healthy mind patterns by instructing us what kinds of things to think about. When we think about those good things, when we meditate on them, the God of peace will be with us. Sign me up for that! What a promise, and it all begins with having gratitude in our minds.

Make a joyful shout to the Lord, all you lands! Serve the Lord with gladness; come before His presence with singing. Know that the Lord, He is God; it is He who has made us, and not we ourselves; we are His people and the sheep of His pasture. Enter into His gates with thanksgiving, and into His courts with praise. Be thankful to Him, and bless His name. For the Lord is good; His mercy is everlasting, and His truth endures to all generations.

Psalm 100

BE THANKFUL, EVEN IN TRIALS

Giving thanks always for all things to God the Father in the name of our Lord Jesus Christ...

Ephesians 5:20

The admonition in the above verse is to be thankful in all things. How can you be thankful in tragedy? You must look for something to be thankful for. When my grandparents died, I was thankful that I'd had them in my life, thankful that I knew they loved me, thankful for a family to lean on in a time of grief, and thankful that I knew they were in heaven with Jesus. I realize that not every grieving person has those types of things to be thankful for. If that is your case, precious soul, be thankful that you have a God walking beside you and supplying everything you'll need to cope with your situation. We must take God's Word and apply it to our everyday circumstances. That means in everything, we thank God. We all need a little practice in this area, but thanksgiving is mandatory, not optional, in the life of the Christian. Keep your eyes wide open and look for the many things you have to be thankful for!

It doesn't matter what your trial is, why you are in it, or how severe it is. God can use all things for your sake. He can take your situation and use it to bring you to a place of thanksgiving, which ultimately brings glory to him. So never give up! No matter how much you may deteriorate on the outside, God is building you up on the inside. You'll be better in the end for having gone through this difficult experience. Everything on earth, no matter how painful, is temporary in the light of eternity because you're not paying attention to the things the world may see—you're looking for the things that will matter in eternity.

Oh, if God's people would just be thankful no matter what comes their way. I don't have any idea what Lance Armstrong, famous for multiple Tour de France victories, believes spiritually. He does, however, get the whole gratitude concept. After being diagnosed with cancer, he fiercely battled it and won. Many of his greatest cycling victories came after his battle with cancer. He has been quoted to say that cancer was the best thing to ever happen to him. Following is a quote spoken at a luncheon sponsored by M.D. Anderson Cancer Center in Houston, Texas.

> The illness is the best thing that ever happened to me. I am lucky to have gone through that, and I would never have won…one Tour de France if I had never been sick. There is no doubt.
>
> —Lance Armstrong

Lance Armstrong has said that the diagnosis of cancer changed his priorities and his perspective and he owes his success to cancer. He made a decision to battle aggressively against this disease, keep a positive attitude, and embrace it as something that could make him a better person and athlete. That's one reason his story has a happy ending. I don't write this to condemn someone who has not beaten cancer after a hard fight. Sometimes we do everything right and still lose. But cancer patients, or anyone in a health crisis, should take note of Lance Armstrong's example. Cancer is an enemy to fight, most assuredly, but as you fight this enemy, take note of how God can use it to make you a stronger, better person, at least on the inside. For that we must be thankful.

We've established that trials can come for a variety of reasons.

Our goal is to let God use our trials to make us better. I'm a fan of outdoor gas grilling. I love how I don't have a hot kitchen or a skillet to clean when I cook a meal outside on the grill. Each time I turn on the grill to preheat it, the grill is covered with the remnants of the last meal I cooked. If I scraped the grill before I turned the heat on, it would be a time-consuming, tedious task, and I still wouldn't get it very clean. But if I just let the grill preheat, the fire will burn off all the leftover crud from the last grilling. In the same way, our God is a consuming fire. We all have crud that needs to be burned out of our lives. Maybe it's selfishness, pride in our own moral excellence, or good works with wrong motives. No Christian escapes the scrutiny of the Holy Spirit. The book of Hebrews has a passage that might be applied to this line of thought. Notice that the writer says in the NIV translation that we should be thankful in this type of situation.

> At that time his voice shook the earth, but now he has promised, "Once more I will shake not only the earth but also the heavens." The words "once more" indicate the removing of what can be shaken—that is, created things—so that what cannot be shaken may remain. Therefore, since we are receiving a kingdom that cannot be shaken, let us be thankful, and so worship God acceptably with reverence and awe, for our "God is a consuming fire."
>
> Hebrews 12:26–29 (NIV)

Oh, saint of God, let your trial be the fire that God uses to purge impurities from you. No matter how painful the process, the end result—the end intended by the Lord—will make you a beauty to behold in your Creator's eyes. For that you can give him praise—and thanks!

TRIAL ONE: IGNORING THE SPIRIT

Do not quench the Spirit.

1 Thessalonians 5:19

On the spiritual level, inner conflict is the warning of the Spirit of God.

—Oswald Chambers

Our young lives were about to take an exciting and drastic turn. We had been married for just over two years, we had an infant son, and Buddy's former high school football coach had just offered him a great-paying job in the oil fields of southeastern Kansas. We were convinced that it was our ticket out of our small town that, in our naïve, youthful minds, offered nothing to our family.

We believed our tiny dollhouse of a home would surely sell quickly once we moved to Coffeyville, Kansas—about a two-hour drive away from our Oklahoma hometown. My whole life I had heard how renting was "throwing your money away," so I determined we should buy a home in Kansas. With excellent credit and a good amount of equity in our home, a second mortgage on our dollhouse was not a problem. Our plan was to buy a home in Coffeyville using the loan money to make the down payment and then pay off the loan once our dollhouse sold. So we set out to find our new home in Kansas with most of our friends and family well aware of our plans—as word gets around quick in a small town.

We found a nice gentleman Realtor in Coffeyville who showed us a few homes and gave us a tour of the town. We fell in love with a home in a new subdivision on the outskirts of town. It was a nice brick home on an acre lot; it was perfect, and we wanted it. We left that weekend with the intentions of returning later to buy it.

Arriving back in our hometown, we enthusiastically described the house we intended to buy to our family and friends. We were prideful about it and excited to think we'd be living in an almost-new home as Buddy started a career that promised a high income, especially for someone just turning twenty-one with only a high school diploma. Everything looked promising. But I didn't *feel* right. I couldn't explain it, so I asked myself, *Am I just nervous? Is the Lord warning me?* I didn't have peace in the situation, but I was too prideful to tell anyone—even my own husband.

We went back to Coffeyville for a final look at our dream home. I had a sick feeling in the pit of my stomach, but my fleshly desire of wanting a new home for my family kept me from giving it the attention it deserved. I considered telling Buddy maybe we should not buy the house, but all I could think about were all the people we had told about the new home. I pushed the uneasy feeling away and allowed pride to keep my mouth shut. Ignoring the still, small voice that spoke to my spirit, I signed my name next to Buddy's on the real estate contract in October of 1981.

Ignoring that uncomfortable feeling was one of the worst decisions of my life. Everything appeared to be in place for a bright future for Buddy and me in Coffeyville. We had no clue that disaster was lurking just around the corner. We now owned two homes and had two regular house payments and a second mortgage. We were two prideful young adults with one tiny baby, one new job, and one big mess about to start.

In the 1970s, the economy of the United States was shaken up by the ramifications of the Arab oil embargo, which created gas shortages and long lines at the gas pumps. But the impact didn't hit Oklahoma, Texas, and Kansas quite as hard since their state economies were largely based on oil production—and it had kicked into high gear. The embargo sent the oil patch into another heyday until the early 1980s when an oil bust and its domino effect crashed down and struck us all.

By the spring of 1982, Buddy's job in oil-well logging was over. He was laid off when the company shut down operations in the Coffeyville area. They offered to transfer him to another section of the country, but already owning two homes, we couldn't afford to pay for another place to live. We had to live in one of our houses and find jobs quickly. Coffeyville's economy was based largely on oil, farming, and the railroad, and they were all in economic trouble. The real estate market was flooded with homes for sale as people left town to find work. Our new home in Coffeyville was just one of many for sale, and we couldn't give the thing away, so to speak.

I'm ashamed to say that my prideful attitude complicated Buddy's devastation at losing his job. The day he was laid off, he was almost distraught wondering how in the world he was going to make ends meet and where he might find work. He told me that we should move back to our hometown, where people knew us and we could both find jobs. I completely balked at that idea. "No!" I cried. "That would be like going home with our tails tucked between our legs! We'll look like failures. I won't do it! You'll just have to find another job here! I'm not going back home."

Silence filled our living room. Buddy lay still on the couch with his arm across his eyes. I sat defiantly on the floor next to him with my jaw set and my arms folded across my chest. He turned to look at me with a loving yet pleading look in his eyes, and he firmly said, "Honey, you don't understand. There are no jobs here for me; we've got to go home. If I've ever needed support, I need yours now."

His words melted my heart and caused me to flinch at the revelation of the ugly, arrogant pride and selfishness that I had just expressed to the husband that I adored. I threw myself into his arms and apologized. "I'll do whatever you say, I'll go wherever you go, and I will not let this ruin our love for each other."

We telephoned our families that afternoon. They drove up in their pickup trucks two days later, and by the end of that week, we had moved back into our little dollhouse.

The consequences of ignoring the Holy Spirit's warning cost us a great amount of money, not to mention the stress and the time it robbed me of spending with my little son since I had to work a full-time job to help make ends meet. For the next two years, we were financially strapped trying to keep the bills paid and our family fed. The real estate market was disastrous in both areas, and we couldn't sell either one of the two houses we owned. Time passed, and we struggled with the consequences of our situation. God eventually led us out of that whole ordeal, but not before we learned a few valuable lessons that I'm so thankful for.

I'm most thankful for learning to not ignore the Holy Spirit. I continue to struggle with stubborn pride as I try to conquer it in my life, but when the Holy Spirit is urging me to go in one direction or another, I dare not ignore him, for I know that there can be severe consequences if I do. I realize now how things would have turned out so differently if we had not purchased a home in Coffeyville. I do believe it was God's will for us to move there, but it was not his will for us to buy another home. Had we only rented, we may have actually saved some money and been in decent financial shape when the job came to an end.

This trial also makes me thankful because I learned not to borrow what I can't pay back! I learned that I cannot count on any income we might have today to be there tomorrow, so don't borrow against it. That is a simple enough lesson, yet it's so seldom learned in our materialistic society.

Another reason I'm so very thankful for the experience of this trial is because the financial disaster—of our own doing—forced us both to our knees. Prior to our poor financial decision, we had been very self-sufficient, even as young as we were. Buddy earned a good wage, and we had more than enough to live on. But when Buddy suddenly lost his job and we had two houses to make payments on and maintain, we were in big trouble. We were forced to trust God every week to provide enough money to pay the bills and eat. That totally changed my prayer life. We had a baby to provide for, and I was very nervous about our new responsibility. I begged and pleaded with God to send a buyer for one of our houses. He didn't send one. This all occurred in the height of the "Name it, Claim it" charismatic movement, and I was naming and claiming every day. I also bound the devil and rebuked him every day. Still, nothing changed for Buddy and me—except our hearts. Our needs pushed us into an area of intimacy and communion with God—and even with each other—that was new to both of us. No, God didn't send a buyer for either one of our homes, but he provided for our every need during that time. Buddy and I both found jobs immediately. The miraculous part of the story is that—on black and white paper—we did not earn enough money to meet our financial obligations and still be able to eat, yet we never missed a payment or a meal. The only explanation is that God supplied our every need.

> Then you shall call, and the Lord will answer; you shall cry, and He will say, "Here I am."
>
> Isaiah 58:9

While a buyer for one of our homes never showed up, God showed up at our home every day. I cried out to God every day for a financial miracle in the form of selling a house. In my cries to the Lord, he answered beyond my best imaginations. He did not answer in the manner I pleaded for, which was a buyer or a financial windfall. Instead, he simply met our needs and gave us more of himself. Money is nice, and I certainly don't mind having some of it. But I'll take more of God over more money any day.

I take full responsibility for our financial mess because at the time, I had more spiritual maturity and training than my good husband and I should have known better than to ignore the Spirit's warning. Instead of listening and obeying God, I used my influence over my husband to lead him into a bad decision. I hadn't yet learned the importance of submitting to my husband, and I thought my plans and ideas were always right. In spite of my willful disobedience, God used this financial crisis to lead Buddy to rededicate his life to Jesus and begin a journey of daily walking with him. God grew my man into a man of God who is so careful to listen to the leading of the Holy Spirit in his daily decisions for our family. That's one more reason why I am thankful God allowed this trial in our lives.

The ninety-first Psalm is a chapter that many Christians quote as a source of divine protection, which I think is fine. However, I don't think you can claim divine protections as offered in Psalm 91—and still remain safe—if you ignore the Holy Spirit's warnings. I remember talking to my beloved pastor, Bro. Ed McGavock, about this situation. I was naming and claiming and believing for a miraculous change in our financial situation. I rebuked demons. I prayed and asked God to deliver us. I stood in faith. I followed all the formulas being taught from pulpits at that time—and none of them worked for me. I didn't know what to do next or where to turn. I was upset and confused as to why nothing was changing. It was in that state of mind that I asked Bro. Ed, "Why did God let this happen? The enemy is stealing from me!" Bro. Ed had a response that I believe came straight from the Holy Spirit: "Did God tell you to buy that house in Coffeyville?" he asked. Right then, I was convicted. I knew this mess was of my own doing because I had felt a check in my spirit. But I insisted on buying instead of renting. I refused to change my mind because of pride. My point boils down to this: having faith for your protection works hand in hand with walking in the Spirit. If God tells you to turn right and you turn left, don't blame him—or anyone else—if trouble is lurking down the left-hand road. It was a good thing when I learned to take responsibility for my own trial and stop pointing fingers at others or whining about being under attack from the devil.

I'm also thankful for this trial since it taught me to appreciate the blessings right under my own nose. At twenty-one years of age, Buddy and I both were chomping at the bit to get out of town and make something of ourselves. We envisioned a big world out there that beckoned us to come and enjoy its various experiences and sights to see as opposed to our hometown of fifteen hundred people where everyone knew your name—and your business. We also looked down our noses at our old ugly Main Street and the run down houses in the city blocks. We complained about having only two places in town for eating out, only one of which offered indoor tables. While in Coffeyville, we had to trust our baby with strangers when we were forced to find a babysitter. The church we attended in Coffeyville had friendly smiles and handshakes, but no one ever contacted us or befriended us while we were there. When I shopped at the grocery store or made a bank deposit, no one knew my name and few said hello. After settling in back home, suddenly the scales fell from my eyes and I saw everything—and everyone—in my hometown in a whole new perspective.

Indeed, I was looking through fresh eyes. We moved home in the spring, and the dogwood trees had never looked so beautiful. I realized how much I missed—and now appreciated—casual conversations and friendly smiles at the post office and the bank. I had forgotten how nice it was to go to a baseball game and cheer for young boys that I had watched grow up. I realized how important it was to raise my child in a town where I knew people would love him simply because he was my child—and gladly offer to babysit at a moment's notice. We were home, and for the first time in my life I appreciated it and I liked it. Like Dorothy in *The Wizard of Oz,* I realized there truly was no place like home.

Oh, how I praise the Lord for what he taught me in that trial. I'm so thankful that I'm not the same as I was before that experience. What an awesome God I serve, who can take my sinful mistake of ignoring his Holy Spirit and use it to make me a more thankful person who is grateful for the blessings I'm surrounded with and for the life lessons learned.

TRIAL TWO: SCARED TO LIFE

For God has not given us a spirit of fear, but of power and of love and of a sound mind.

2 Timothy 1:7

Buddy held his lunchbox under his arm as he kissed me good-bye at our front door. He was leaving to go work the midnight shift at the Carbide plant. Locking the door behind him, I could hear the snow crunching under his feet as he walked to his pickup. I took a deep breath and looked around at the household chores I'd neglected all day. Our second baby was due anytime, and I had felt mild contractions that kept me lying down most of the day and evening. But now the contractions had stopped. I had a fresh burst of energy and decided it would be wise to take advantage of it and get my little house in order while I felt good. I peeked in Andy's room and saw him fast asleep in his waterbed. I pulled his teddy bear sheets and blue blanket up over his little shoulders then bent down to kiss his forehead. He was almost four years old and was an absolute joy to his daddy and me. I gathered Andy's clothes from his hamper and headed to the laundry. While a load of clothes was agitating in the washing machine, I straightened up the rest of the house then headed for the kitchen to tackle a sink full of dirty dishes—my final and most dreaded chore.

When the clock chimed one o'clock, I realized just how exhausted I was, and I was anxious to go to bed. I finished loading the dishwasher and started to scrub the cast-iron frying pan when all of a sudden there was a loud pounding noise at my back door! My heart jumped at the sound of what I thought was someone trying to break in! I turned and ran out of the kitchen, bumping my pregnant belly into the stove as I went. I rushed to the bedroom telephone to call my daddy, who lived up the street. I had most of his phone number dialed when I remembered that Momma and Daddy were out of town. I tried to get a grip and calm myself down. I hadn't heard any noises in a couple of minutes, so I rationalized that it could be the wind blowing the screen door. I decided to be brave and go back to the kitchen to check on the back door. As I stepped onto the vinyl floor of the kitchen, I immediately saw the red indicator light on my stove. When I had bumped into it, I had accidentally turned on a burner. I reached for the knob and turned the burner off, thankful that nothing was on the stove to catch fire. Then I took a step toward the door. I just needed to look out the window of the back door and see if the screen was unlatched. I reached a shaky hand toward the doorknob when the door began pounding again.

At this point, I was frantic and convinced someone was outside. I ran to Andy's room, and despite my pregnant condition, I lifted him out of his bed and awkwardly carried him to my bedroom. He was in a sound sleep and didn't wake up as I strained to bend over and gently lay him on my bed. I hurried to Buddy's gun cabinet and grabbed his shotgun, loaded it, and sat, terrified, on the edge of my waterbed. With my heart pounding and my thoughts racing, I just sat there in my long flannel gown. If I had been absolutely certain it was a break-in attempt, I would have called the police, but I wasn't sure and I didn't want to risk the embarrassment if it turned out to just be the wind blowing an unlatched screen door. I debated in my mind what to do next. I decided to call my next-door neighbor, even though I didn't know him very well. I rationalized that if the noise was just my door banging in the wind, it would be better to risk embarrassment with just my neighbor, as opposed to the whole town hearing about it if I called the police.

My neighbor answered his phone. I apologized for calling at such a late hour, and I tried to downplay my fear when I asked him to look outside for me from the vantage point of his back porch. He assured me it was no problem for him to go outside and check—he was awake and watching late night TV anyway. He called me back in a few moments to tell me that it must be the wind because there were no footprints in the snow at our back door. I thanked him and apologized once again for causing him inconvenience so late on a wintry night. I set the telephone back into its receiver and tried to shake off the intense feeling of fear that had a grip on me.

Okay, this is crazy, I told myself. *It's just the wind blowing the door; go in there and turn off the kitchen light; then go to bed.* That's what I told myself to do, but I didn't know if I had the courage to do it. I unloaded the shotgun and crept back to the kitchen, terrified to go back in there. I mustered the courage to try. Just as I entered the kitchen, the door banged loudly again! I ran back to my bedroom, called Buddy at work, and through hysterical tears, I insisted he come home right away.

"Honey, I can't leave work just because you're scared!" Buddy said. I had told him the whole story, and he explained that he had not latched the back door earlier that evening and he was certain it was the wind blowing the door. At this point, my mind was no longer sound or rational, and I started to have strong contractions while crying on the phone. Buddy sighed and promised to come home right away.

When Buddy arrived home, he made me go to the back door with him so he could prove to me that no one had been there. The cold air hit my face when I looked outside, where the moonlight was reflecting off the drift of snow over our back steps. It was undisturbed. Not a single footprint anywhere. Humiliated, I looked at Buddy and cried again. Not only had I been upset for no reason, but my fear demanded Buddy leave work, and that had cost us most of a day's pay—and we certainly couldn't afford to lose any wages. We put Andy back in his bed, Buddy got into the shower, and finally feeling safe, I was asleep in minutes.

My story doesn't sound like a major trial of life, does it? On the surface, it absolutely is not. It might even be something I could laugh about today, if not for what happened that night on a spiritual level. Even I didn't fully comprehend what happened that night until sometime later. That frightful night for me was the beginning of a trial that not only adversely affected me, but also my children.

A few days after my night of fear, on the eighth of February, Sarah Jane "Janie" Holman was born to us. Buddy's shift work schedule allowed him to be home at night when we first brought her home from the hospital. I was thankful for my healthy baby, and life was great—until Buddy had to work another midnight shift. In fact, Buddy's work schedule changed, and for the first time in our married lives, he was working only midnight shifts. Each night he left for work, I lived in unwarranted and debilitating fear.

I lived in this fear for the next several years. This was not a mild type of fear that many women feel when they are alone. I lived in constant fear and even terror whenever Buddy was away at night. I would try to go to bed and sleep, but every sound was startling and made me jump. I walked through our house at night, peeking out the mini blinds to see if someone was lurking outside. I had triple locks on all the doors and still pulled chairs in front of them at night. I slept with a shotgun by my bed, laid open on the floor, with the shotgun shells standing ready on my nightstand for quick loading.

I can't explain in enough detail just how afraid I was to be home at night without Buddy. I believed it was up to me to protect myself and our babies from the evils that could hurt us. I felt exposed and helpless. Living in this pitiful condition, the days and months dragged on until it began to take a toll on me physically and mentally. I seldom slept through the night, and exhaustion was a continual state for me. The fatigue began to affect my mental health. I put my sweet husband through sheer torture every night, as he would leave for work with me crying and begging him not to go. I was terrified of what harm might come to the kids and me from evil people outside. I was about to learn that the evil was not outside, but living with us in our little dollhouse.

This part of the story may be difficult for some readers to believe or understand, but I believe that on the night the wind banged my back door, a demonic spirit entered my home. I had clues of this from the beginning but wasn't spiritually knowledgeable enough at the time to recognize them and then to know what to do about it. My first clue was in Sarah Jane's sleeping patterns. She slept through the night quite well as a baby—except when Buddy worked the midnight shifts. Buddy's work schedule had returned to rotating shifts of days, evenings, and midnights. Every time Buddy worked a midnight shift, she awoke screaming in the night. During the other shifts, she slept straight through all night. Another clue I overlooked were the unexplained noises that would wake me up at night once I'd finally gotten Sarah Jane back to sleep. I would hear things and jump up out of bed to investigate, only to find nothing—except another long night of terrifying fear, praying for sweet sleep to take me to daybreak.

Perhaps it was just the fatigue taking a toll on me mentally, but there were times when it seemed as though something in my house was laughing at me. I know this sounds like I'm a "straight runnin' nut"—as we say in Oklahoma—but believe me, it was real to me. I would lay in bed alone at night, breathing very shallowly, straining my ears to hear anything that might indicate danger, and I could feel something laughing at me. It seemed to me that this "spirit" was mocking me as if to say, "And you think you're a strong Christian! Look at you! You have no power to conquer fear!" I wish I could better explain this, but you'll just have to believe me when I say I was being tormented by something in my own home.

The biggest clue that pointed to something demonic in my house actually turned out to be evidence I was too ignorant to see. Buddy was working an evening shift, and I expected him home just after midnight. At about eight in the evening, I had just put Sarah Jane to bed and was helping Andy wind up his bedtime routine. There was a TV movie coming on that I wanted to watch, so I hurried Andy along to bed before it started. I tucked him in and went to the living room to watch my movie and fold some laundry. The movie started, and I just wanted to escape into it so I could forget my own troubles. About fifteen minutes into my movie, Andy came walking down the hall toward me. He wanted another drink of water, like little children do when they really don't want to go to bed. I gave him a drink and sent him back down the long hall toward his bedroom, which was directly across the hall from our bedroom. Just as Andy reached the point in the hallway that was between both bedroom doors, he let out a horrible scream and ran to me. His face was already full of tears, and I could see the terror in his eyes. "Mommy, I just saw the devil in your room!"

One of the biggest regrets of my life was that I did not believe or perceive what my frightened little boy actually saw. All I could think about was the aggravation of having my movie interrupted. I told him the devil was not in my room, and I even walked him in there to prove it to him. He returned to the living room with me, where I held him until he calmed down. After a short while, I sent him back to his bed. Upon reaching the same point in the hall, Andy turned and ran straight back to me. He had seen it again! By this point—I'm ashamed to admit—I was just plain aggravated that he wouldn't go to bed. I scolded him and sent him down the hall. I watched him run with his head down into his bedroom, and he didn't come out again. That was the end of that. I never thought about it again, and he never mentioned it again—until sixteen years later.

Andy was always an obedient child and not one to question what Mommy and Daddy said. He never talked about what he saw that night until he was twenty-two years old. He reminded me of that night, which I remembered clearly, and he described in vivid detail a small, reddish colored being about his size that stared at him twice from a corner in my bedroom. He said that after that night he never looked in my room again when he walked down the hall, and he certainly never came in my room at night. He was so affected by what he saw that a few years later he offered to trade his larger bedroom for his sister's smaller one just so he wouldn't have to be that close to my room.

When Andy reminded me of that dreadful night, it took all my strength to not break down in front of him. My selfishness and lack of spiritual knowledge and perception had cost my son years of torment. It still breaks my heart today to know how scared he was as a little boy, and I didn't do anything to help calm his fears, let alone even acknowledge that they were real and justified.

I lived with that tormenting spirit in my house for about five years. Every night before bed, I would read my Bible and pray. I would ask God to station angels around our house and around our beds to protect us from the enemy. I would beg God every night to give me a peaceful night's sleep. I started rebuking the devil. For five long years, nothing changed. Then two things happened almost simultaneously.

Fran is my longtime friend and mentor. We attended church together for over thirty years. One Sunday morning during the middle of an anointed worship service, Fran walked over to me and said, "Lorraine, I don't want you to live in fear anymore." She laid her hands on me and prayed, asking the Lord to deliver me from my fear. I felt so peaceful when she finished praying, and I believed God was going to help me overcome the fear I'd been living in. About the same time as Fran's prayer, I came across a passage in Proverbs that was life changing to me. Buddy was working another midnight shift, and I was hoping to make it through just one more night. I placed my Bible on the couch in my living room and got down on my knees to pray. After asking God to help me to sleep and not be afraid, I opened the Word of God and it fell open to the book of Proverbs.

> My son, let them not depart from your eyes—keep sound wisdom and discretion; so they will be life to your soul and grace to your neck. Then you will walk safely in your way, and your foot will not stumble. When you lie down, you will not be afraid; yes, you will lie down and your sleep will be sweet. Do not be afraid of sudden terror, nor of trouble from the wicked when it comes; for the

Lord will be your confidence, and will keep your foot from being caught.

Proverbs 3:21–26

My heart leapt upon reading these words. I felt as though the Lord was speaking words of comfort directly to my troubled and tormented soul. I was excited at the promise of lying down and not being afraid and having sweet sleep, but as applicable as those words were to my condition, they were not the phrases that had the most impact on me. It was the tiny little word of *when* that jumped off the page at me. God was telling me not to be afraid of trouble from the wicked *when* it came! Now it would stand to reason that for a woman already living in fear, those words would scare her even more, knowing that trouble from the wicked *would* come in some form or another. But that's not how the Holy Spirit revealed it to me that night. I believed the Lord was assuring me that when trouble from the wicked came, he would be my confidence and would not let it ultimately destroy me. I can't tell you the peace that came upon my heart. Finally, I realized that it wasn't up to me to protect myself and my children; God would do it! Yes, trouble might come, but God would not let it destroy me. It might scare me, it might even hurt my family or me, but it would not destroy me because my confidence was in him, not in my own self-sufficiency. I knew that whatever happened in my life, God would walk me through it and I would see victory, however God defined it, and glory would be brought to his name.

After taking time to worship the Lord right in my living room, dressed in my jammies, I got up off my knees and looked right at my front door. The main door was tripled locked, with a storm door on the outside also locked, and I had a chair pulled in front of it as well. I looked at that door with the strangest feeling of confidence. It was as if I almost dared wickedness to come on in; I wasn't afraid of it, and I was ready for battle because the Lord would fight for me! The dread of evil was gone. I felt delivered, and I felt safe in the protective arms of my strong Deliverer.

From that point forward, my life began to change dramatically as I learned to live a life without tormenting fear. Gone were the days when I was too afraid to take a shower even in the daytime if I were home alone. Gone were the days of turning our thermostat to a degree where it would not kick on at night because I was afraid of not hearing potentially threatening noises from outdoors. Gone were the days of locking my house up like Fort Knox when Buddy was at work. And gone were the nights when I just longed for the break of day. I was set free, and I knew it! In those days we sang an Albert E. Brumley chorus at our church that always brought me to my feet: "He set me free, yes, He set me free. He broke the bonds of prison for me."

I don't know what happened to the demonic being that Andy saw in my bedroom. I don't know if it left my house completely or if it chose another target besides me to torment. I'll just have to wait until I get to heaven to find out, and I'm not sure it will even matter to me at that point.

I'm just so thankful that I'm not a scaredy-cat anymore. Sometimes I've been amazed at how far the Lord has brought me. We eventually moved out of our little dollhouse and bought a home that had once belonged to an elderly couple who were old family friends of ours. In fact, with a Bible on his lap, the husband passed away in the living room of the home we bought. For me to be able to live in a house that someone had died in would have been a far stretch of the imagination just a few years before. But at the time we moved, I had a new understanding, and the devil couldn't use old tactics to scare this ol' gal any longer! In fact, I reasoned to myself, *Why be afraid to live in a house where angels have been as they escorted a saint of God to his heavenly home?*

I'm so thankful for the experience of this time of fear because life is filled with opportunities to be afraid. I know what it's like to have fear dominate your very existence, and I refuse to live in that condition any longer. When the enemy tries to scare me, I've learned to capture my thoughts and imaginations and refuse to succumb to my old way of living. I'll admit that this can still be a battle for me when I'm home alone. But since I've tasted the sweetness of victory,

I'll fight with the full armor of God so I never taste the bitterness of defeat again. If I'd never experienced such fear, I would never know the powerful deliverance of my God. No one can convince me that the blood of Jesus and the Word of God don't have delivering power because I'm living proof of it.

I feel like the servant of Elisha in 2 Kings 6 who had his spiritual eyes opened. In a surprise move, the mighty Syrian army came at night and completely surrounded the city where the Prophet Elisha and his servant were sleeping. When the servant awoke early in the morning, he saw the Syrian army with its horses and chariots standing ready to attack at any moment. With panic in his voice, the servant asked Elisha, "What shall we do?" Elisha gave a calm, assuring response to his terrified servant, saying, "Do not fear, for those who are with us are more than those who are with them." Then Elisha asked the Lord to open the eyes of his servant. In answer to Elisha's prayer, the Lord opened the spiritual eyes of the servant, and he saw a mountain filled with horses and chariots of fire all around Elisha. What a sight that must have been! In seeing the heavenly hosts of protection surrounding them, the once-fearful servant must have experienced a sense of protection and peace.

That was exactly how I felt when God delivered me. I didn't see anything to indicate supernatural protection, but I was confident it was there. Like Elisha's once-frightened servant, my own spiritual eyes had also been opened, and I understood that my God had me surrounded. I could plainly see that those who were with me were more than those who were with them!

Dear brother or sister, if your trial involves fear, know that whatever comes your way, the Lord will not let your foot be caught. He will walk you through the most frightening of evils and be your Deliverer. Whatever comes, he will not let it ultimately destroy you. I also encourage you to ask your heavenly Father to open your own spiritual eyes so that you may see that while in the natural you are surrounded by evil, in the spiritual you are also surrounded by a more powerful, fiery army just waiting to defend you. So never fear, and be thankful because you're surrounded.

TRIAL THREE: "GOD, I'M SO MAD AT YOU!"

And let the peace of God rule in your hearts, to which also you were called in one body; and be thankful.

Colossians 3:15

I looked out the picture window to check on Andy as he played in our front yard. It was an unusually warm day for January, and my four-and-a-half-year-old little boy was delighted to play outdoors after being cooped up in the house because of cold weather. I watched him carefully, even though the majority of our yard offered protection with a fence. Before letting Andy go outside, I had reminded him of our rules—rules I had drilled into him for months. Andy knew about the importance of staying in the yard, never talking to strangers, and never, never going near the fence that was between us and our neighbors with the pit bull dogs. Our neighbors were nice people and good to us, but their dogs frightened me. Anytime we approached the chain-link fence that bordered our property lines, those dogs ferociously charged the fence line and barked at us.

Andy never attempted to go near the dangerous side of our yard since he developed a fear of dogs the year before. At that time, I was pregnant with our daughter and Andy wanted to go for a ride on my bicycle, so my mom rode him around the neighborhood. Andy was so excited to ride behind Grandma in the kiddy seat, and they were having a great time together—until a pack of dogs began to chase them. My mom tried to outrun them, but while she was pedaling as fast as she could, one of the dogs—a pit bull—bit her on her calf muscle. Even with the dog holding its gripping bite on her, she continued to ride the bike, fearing that if she stopped she couldn't protect Andy. The dog finally let go, and Momma sped away, getting them both to safety. She reported the attack to the police department, who monitored the dog for rabies and then had it put down. Her physical wounds healed, but Andy carried the emotional wound of that frightful day. From that day on, he had a fear of dogs—until that January day I watched him playing outdoors.

I stepped away from the picture window so I could check on Sarah Jane, who was napping in her crib. When I looked back outside to check on Andy, I was both cautious and surprised when I saw him playing with a strange dog in our yard! I ran outside to make sure he was okay, and when I did, the little white Samoyed dog darted away from Andy. "Look, Mommy! A doggie came to play with me!" Andy shouted excitedly. I was amazed that Andy wasn't afraid of this little dog, but the little dog was certainly afraid of me.

We determined that the dog was a stray—not unusual in our rural town without leash laws—and she had likely been abused by adults. She wouldn't come near Buddy or me, but she adored Andy. Whether she adopted us or we adopted her, I'm not sure, but she became our dog. We named her Daisy, and her sweet disposition helped Andy overcome his fear of dogs. She obediently stayed in our yard, and she seemed to instinctively know to stay away from the fence that separated us from the pit bulls with the nasty attitudes.

On the days that the weather cooperated, Andy would play outside all day with Daisy. Andy picked out chew toys for Daisy, and he taught her to play fetch. My boy loved this little dog with his whole heart. On several occasions, I looked out our picture window to see Andy, bundled up in his tiny coveralls and stocking cap, just lying contentedly on the cold ground next to Daisy, petting her soft white fur.

I believed the Lord had sent this sweet little dog to help Andy overcome his fear of dogs. And he certainly did. He was never afraid of dogs after loving Daisy. Daisy slowly began to trust Buddy and me, and after just a month of being in our family, we all loved her.

One afternoon, I drove into our yard to find Daisy surrounded by several male dogs. Apparently they were all interested in being her boyfriend—if you know what I mean. Buddy took Daisy to the vet's office right away to remedy her condition. We didn't want puppies, and we didn't want strange dogs coming into our yard. After Daisy's procedure at the vet's office, Buddy brought her home and we got her settled into her little bed on our front porch. Daisy was an outside dog, and we didn't expect any complications. We checked on her throughout the day, noticing her slow movements and sympathizing with her discomfort. At bedtime, Andy petted her, fed her, filled her water bowl, and said his good night to her.

Buddy checked on Daisy one last time and kissed me good-bye as he left to work a midnight shift—again. This was during the time when I lived in paralyzing fear at night. I snuggled in bed on the cold winter night and eventually drifted off to sleep. Suddenly, I heard dogs barking. I jumped out of bed and hurried to the picture window that overlooked the porch where Daisy's bed was. She was still lying on her bed, her teeth snarled, snapping and barking at the male dogs that surrounded her on our porch. She had been spayed that day, but there must have been a scent remaining on her that had the male dogs interested, while she was definitely not interested.

I knocked on the window, trying to shoo away the sniffing, barking dogs. It was only a partial remedy. They left the porch and stood in the yard just a short distance away. Every time I tried to go back to bed, the situation repeated itself. The dogs would surround

Daisy, and she would snap at them, trying to fight them off. I would beat on the wall or window, trying to scare them away, and it would only keep them away for moments. Looking back, I wish I had had the courage to open the door and bring her in the house, but I'd never had a house dog and presumed she wasn't housebroken. Two or three long hours passed in the night, and I repeatedly tried to protect Daisy from inside the house. Finally, I decided I just couldn't do it any longer; I was exhausted and needed to go to sleep. Before I headed back to bed, I asked the Lord to protect Daisy. I remember praying, "Lord, I put Daisy in your hands. Please guard and protect her while I go to sleep." I went to bed that night trusting that God would keep those dogs away from Daisy and that the morning would find both Daisy and me rested. But morning did not bring rest; it brought horror and heart-wrenching grief.

The sun was shining through my bedroom window when I awoke to the sounds of dogs barking. But this wasn't ordinary barking; it sounded scary and frantic, almost like wild animals out of control. Throwing the blankets off, I ran to my bedroom window, and what I saw sent me into a panic. There were a pack of dogs fighting in the street, and Daisy was in the yard next door, trying to fight off the pit bulls! She was between them—literally being pulled apart by them. I lifted my long flannel gown up so I could run, and I flew out the front door barefooted. When I got to the steps of our front porch, I saw Daddy in the street in front of our neighbor's house. He was running toward me, waving his arms at me and yelling at me to go back in the house. I stood frozen and in shock at what I was seeing. Daisy's snow-white fur was covered in blood, and she struggled to protect herself from the vicious jaws of the pit bull dogs. By this point, one of her legs had been ripped from her tiny body. Suddenly, I remembered Andy! I did not want him to see his Daisy being torn apart like this.

I ran back into the house just as he was hurrying down the hall in his footed pajamas to meet me. "Mommy, is Daisy okay?" he asked with a quivering lip and fear in his tear-filled blue eyes. Trying to think of an answer that wouldn't upset him, I explained to him that Daisy was very sick and that she was going to die.

"Then why is she next door?" Andy asked. It was then that I knew he had looked out the window and witnessed at least part of the traumatic scene.

"Well," I said, trying to sound convincing, "she went next door to tell those dogs good-bye."

"No!" Andy cried. "Daisy wouldn't do that! She knows those dogs are mean!" Andy burst into tears at the realization that his little Daisy was dying.

By this time, Daddy was coming through the front door. He had been on his way to work that morning when he saw Daisy fighting for her life. He knew his own life would be risked if he went inside the yard, so he angrily kicked the neighbor's garage door, trying to wake them up and get them outside to stop the brutal attack. I sent Andy to his room to dress while Daddy explained all this to me. I asked him about Daisy's condition and if we could save her. With tender compassion in his voice, Daddy explained, "No, baby, she's ripped apart. There's nothing that can be done for her." He went on to say that the neighbor volunteered to put her out of her misery and bury her for us. About that time I heard a single gunshot echo in the still morning air, and I knew little Daisy was completely gone.

Buddy came home from work that morning to find his young family crumpled on the couch, crying. I told him the whole story, and we both vented our frustrations about the neighbors' dangerous dogs and how much more we now feared for our children's safety outdoors. We were also puzzled about how Daisy got in the yard next door. Our yard was not completely fenced, but theirs was. In fact, it had a concrete barrier at the bottom, topped with chain link. Inspecting the fence later that day, we found that it was bent behind our drive-through gate where it met the concrete on our property line. We concluded that Daisy was trying to get away from the pack of dogs that harassed her through the night and she must have wedged herself between the open gate and the fence, where the pit bull dogs were able to grab her and drag her under.

It was one of the saddest days of our lives. Buddy went on to bed to sleep through the day, and I didn't even bother to get dressed after I fed the kids a late-morning breakfast. Sarah Jane was playing contentedly in her room. Andy cried tears over losing Daisy but seemed satisfied with my weak explanation of the morning's events. He was processing in his young mind that his little Daisy was dead and wouldn't be outside waiting to play with him anymore. While I was sitting on the couch staring blankly at the television, Andy walked back in the living room. He stood in front of me, dressed in dark green coveralls and a black and orange knitted facemask that was way too big for him. In his four-year-old arms, he carried an army shovel and Daisy's doggie toys.

"What are you doing?" I asked him, already knowing in my heart what his plans must be.

He looked at me and with a solemn—and quite responsible—tone in his quivering voice, he said, "I'm going outside to bury Daisy's toys."

I threw my arms around him and fought back my own tears. "Honey, you don't have to do that," I told him.

Several minutes later I finally convinced him not to go outside in the cold and bury Daisy's toys. With a sad and confused countenance, he headed back to his room to change clothes.

This was the emotional breaking point for me. When I saw the grief in my baby boy's eyes and how broken his tender heart was, I realized just how mad I was. Mad at the neighbors for having vicious dogs—yes. Mad at myself for not bringing Daisy inside—yes. But mostly I was mad at God! How dare he not answer my pleas to protect Daisy! How could he let my son endure this grief and loss? I had trusted him with my children and with Daisy, and he let me down. Not only had he let me down by not answering my prayers, but he let my little boy suffer. That was what angered me the most. My little boy had a broken heart, and God could have prevented it.

The emotions and attitudes running through my mind were scaring me. If you could have seen my inner person, you would have seen a young woman with squinted eyes, pursed lips, a set jaw, one hand on her hip, and the other pointing a finger in the face of God. I had never felt this way before. Could a Christian be angry with God and not get struck dead immediately? I was an emotional, conflicted mess of a person and not coping well at all with my inner turmoil. I needed time to calm down and think, but my feelings wouldn't get out of the way, especially when I looked at my son's sad little face every time he spoke of how much he was going to miss Daisy.

After a few days, the Holy Spirit began to teach me and illuminate some truths to me. What I learned in the process has made me thankful for the whole experience. I came to realize that as my children grew, I could never shield them enough to prevent them from the experiences of suffering and pain. Life happens to us all, and it brings painful experiences. However, it's those painful experiences that develop character and maturity in us, and without them we would all remain shallow, selfish individuals. I learned that I could trust God to use hardship and pain in the lives of my children, and as they endured the suffering, God would make them better for it.

We lived in that same little dollhouse—with the same neighbors, with the same fence, with the same pit bull dogs—for another ten years. I tell you this to give thanks and glory to God for the protection of my children. Kids shouldn't be kept locked in a house; they need to play outside. If Daisy had not been killed by the ferocious dogs next door, my children may not have comprehended the danger lurking at the fence line and become victims themselves. They grew up without fear and with a healthy respect of the dogs next door. They knew to stay away from that fence. Daisy's life may have been given in place of my own children's lives. Daisy's death certainly hurt, but it cannot compare to the pain of losing a loved human being.

I'm also thankful for the love of God that cannot be exhausted— even by mad mommas. While I was so angry at God, he just kept on loving me, waiting for my head and heart to be still long enough for him to do his work in me. I knew the truth about God—that he loved me and that he loved my son more than even I was capable of. Although I had been taught this truth in multiple Bible lessons, it was now time for me to know this truth on a personal level. I can't tell you how much I've come to learn of the inexhaustible love of God since losing Daisy. No matter what I do, what I say, how I feel, or what happens to me, God's love for me never changes. I did not deserve a love so great that would wrap me in a tender embrace even while I breathed angry accusations at him. God loves with a love beyond imagination even for the most undeserving—and that was (and still is) me. It really is true that "you shall know the truth and the truth shall set you free" (John 8:32). I knew the truth of God's love. Despite my anger, the knowledge of that truth set me free while the circumstances still stared me in the face. My anger dissolved and I was set free once I grasped with my heart what my head already knew—God's love never changes.

Friend, have you ever been angry at God? You are not alone. There's no shame in admitting feelings that God knows you have anyway. Your anger is no surprise to him. Get on your knees and tell him how you feel and then allow him to minister to you. Your human eyes are likely clouded and misinterpreting the whole scene. Momentary feelings are normal and quite understandable. But I beg you not to let the devil catch you in a trap that skews your vision of the nature of God because of the trial that hurts you today.

The New Testament records Jesus telling the parable of the Talents. In this parable, we see a man who was upset with God and refused to see the goodness of God. This man had that skewed vision of God that people in trials need to be on guard for. Don't let the enemy use your pain to turn you away from the Abba Father who wants to hold you and love all your hurt away.

This familiar passage is found in the book of Matthew. In this story, a man gives three of his servants something called *talents,* which were valuable. One servant received five, another received two, and the final servant received one. Jesus explains that the master gave to each servant according to his own ability. After dispensing the talents, the master left on a journey. The first two servants worked to double what had been entrusted to them. The third servant, who was given only one talent, buried his talent in the ground. After a long while, the master returned to find out how his talents were managed by the servants. The first two servants were complimented and rewarded for their good stewardship. The third servant not only approached his master without an increase but with an attitude to boot! Here is his statement:

> Then he who had received the one talent came and said, "Lord, I knew you to be a hard man, reaping where you have not sown, and gathering where you have not scattered seed. And I was afraid, and went and hid your talent in the ground. Look, there you have what is yours.'"
>
> Matthew 25:24–25

The servant accused his master of demanding too much from him. He should have asked forgiveness for his own laziness. The master rebuked the lazy servant for not even depositing the talent with the bankers, where it could have earned interest—no work required! The servant was punished for his uselessness. The question in my mind about this story is, "What caused the servant to be useless—unprofitable?" The obvious answer to me is his attitude.

In *My Utmost for His Highest*, Oswald Chambers says that the servant implied, "I know your intent is to leave me unprotected and vulnerable." His wrong belief paralyzed him with fear and caused him to do nothing and resulted in harsh punishment. His wrong belief contradicted what he should have known, which is that his master was a giving man who entrusted a valuable talent to the servant.

When our little Daisy was killed by the pit bull dogs next door, the trauma caused me to overlook what I knew. I knew God was a good and loving God—all the time. I allowed my hurt to temporarily blind me. My overwhelming emotions resulted in anger at God. I was so mad that God would allow Daisy's death and break the heart of my little boy. Reflecting now on the whole story, yes, it was a sad, hard day. But the knowledge of God's love eventually lifted me out of that trap of anger. I didn't have a vision, I didn't hear an audible voice, and God's finger didn't write on my wall, but God revealed a truth to my heart in those tearful days. He let me know that my sweet little boy and his sister would face much greater trials in their future. He promised me that today's pain would prepare them for tomorrow's pain. He assured me I could trust him with their future. When God dropped this truth into my spirit, I knew it was true. It was a knowledge that would keep me out of bondage in the future when both of my children faced storms in their lives. What a blessing it was to know this as a young mother before I had to witness my offspring face bigger and more hurtful trials. When those bigger trials arrived, I knew to simply trust God and let him work things out for our good. I was able to keep my knowledge of God's love for us at the forefront of my mind when the next trial came, and the next and the next…The reality I'm thankful for is that the dark day of losing our little Daisy actually brought light to my heart. The Lord brought healing to us and instilled in us an ability to face future pain with complete knowledge of his love.

I opened this chapter with Colossians 3:15, where Paul admonished us to let the peace of God rule in our hearts. The Greek word translated *rule* is a word that described someone who judged an athletic contest. When a baseball is hit outside the playing field, the umpire yells, "Foul ball!" When a basketball is thrown out of bounds, the referee blows his whistle to stop play. In a similar way, when you have a wrong belief or wrong reaction to a situation, the peace of God will judge it to be foul or out of the bounds of the truth! When trouble knocks on our doors, our minds and emotions may want to react with anger or depression. That's when we need to let the peace of God rule (judge) the circumstances and make the correct call in regard to our reaction. The call will always be the truth: God is good and you are loved, no matter what is thrown at you. Our job is to let the peace of God rule. For that ruling peace of God in our hearts, we can be most thankful.

Dear one, when your heart is broken, let the peace of God rule in your heart. And when it does, it will cause you to remember what you know. You'll remember that God is good—all the time. Don't let the enemy plant seeds of doubt, bitterness, anger, and mistrust in your hurting heart. Your loving Father hasn't changed—in spite of the pain that surrounds you—and he is waiting with outstretched arms that want to hold you until the pain fades away.

TRIAL FOUR: YOUR GOOD GIRL IS GONNA GO BAD

Thus my heart was grieved, and I was vexed in my mind. I was so foolish and ignorant; I was like a beast before You. Nevertheless I am continually with You; You hold me by my right hand. You will guide me with Your counsel, and afterward receive me to glory. Whom have I in heaven but You? And there is none upon earth that I desire besides You. My flesh and my heart fail; but God is the strength of my heart and my portion forever. For indeed, those who are far from You shall perish; You have destroyed all those who desert You for harlotry. But it is good for me to draw near to God; I have put my trust in the Lord God, that I may declare all Your works.

Psalm 73:21–28

It was suppertime, and the guilt weighed heavy on me because I knew my kids were getting hungry. They had already tippy-toed into my bedroom twice, timidly asking if I was ready to get up yet. I couldn't motivate myself to get out of bed. Buddy was working and wouldn't be home until after midnight. I just lay there consumed with self-pity and self-loathing. I had no energy—and no heart—to get up and take care of my family. I felt like a failure as a wife and a mommy. The tears, which flowed a lot these days, were falling across my face, soaking my pillowcase. I still didn't move. Then I heard the kitchen cabinets opening and closing. The kids must be looking for a snack. I heard a kitchen chair being pulled across the floor, followed by the familiar hum of the electric can opener. The soft clank of metal against metal told me a pan was being placed on the electric burner of the stove. I knew then that the kids were trying to cook supper by themselves. *What a horrible momma I am!* I thought to myself. But I still kept lying there, crying all the more at the thought of forcing my kids to fix their own supper. I don't know how much longer I stayed in bed. Guilt and shame had tried to hold me in that bed, but somewhere deep inside, my concern for Andy and Janie drug me out of my dark bedroom. Children that age should not be near a hot stove.

I walked into the kitchen, fully expecting my children to be disappointed in their neglectful mother. But instead of facing rejection, I found unconditional love in their smiling faces. Andy proudly looked at me and said, "Look, Mommy, we cooked supper for you!" The dishes and silverware were neatly set at the table, and they served a can of warmed pork and beans for the three of us to share. Looking at the meal their loving little hands had prepared made me feel more guilt and shame as I thought, *What kind of mother am I? Don't I care about my children's nutrition?* I hugged them both, told them thanks, and wiped more tears from my swollen eyes. I quickly added more food to our meal, being careful not to hurt their feelings or disparage what their little hands had so graciously prepared.

This was a typical scene from the deep, dark, depressed days when I was plagued with pre-menstrual syndrome, or PMS. Unfortunately, it was the 1980s and the mental and emotional aspects of PMS were not yet as commonly known as they are today. I certainly didn't have a clue as to why I had such drastic mood swings and irrational behavior. I didn't know at the onset of my trouble that I had an explainable—notice I didn't say excusable—condition. While many women experience a few days of mild irritability, my month consisted of about fifteen days of normalcy followed by fifteen days of emotional chaos. The good days were great! I was myself—the good wife and creative, playful mother, the good housekeeper, the conscientious nutritionist for my family. The bad days were spent in fits of angry outbursts over the slightest aggravations, and my mouth was full of hateful criticism, as no one in my young family could do anything right in my eyes. All month long—every month—fatigue and guilt were my constant companions. During the good days, I worked so hard to catch up on my household chores and prepare for the bad days that I knew were right around the corner. During the dark days of the month, I focused only on myself and how bad I felt, both physically and emotionally. Unable to cope with the simplest of stressors, I blamed poor Buddy for everything that irritated me. I accused him of not understanding me and of not offering to help me more with the household chores. Everything the kids did rattled what few nerves I had left. They were normal children—and actually quite well behaved—but to me they were too loud, they made too many messes, and they didn't obey me quickly enough. I was the problem, but I always found a scapegoat to blame in my miserable condition.

The guilt, shame, and feelings of failure added up to a weight that I could no longer bear. I had always been the good girl. I was the girl who did things morally right. I was the one who focused on loving my husband and raising our children to know Jesus. But that young woman had just become her family's worst nightmare! I began pondering how they would be better off without me. Thoughts of suicide plagued me. When I was driving alone, I considered running off the road and into a tree but worried that if I didn't die, the medical bills would bankrupt us. When Buddy worked the midnight shift, I kept a shotgun next to my bed for protection. On one particular night, in the depths of irrational depression, I loaded that gun and contemplated taking my life. I thought Buddy and the kids would be better off without me. I reasoned that Buddy was a great daddy and he could raise our children just fine without me.

The two things I couldn't resolve as I considered pulling the trigger were how a suicide would affect my kids and what God would say when I stood before him. I feared a holy God, and I certainly didn't want my children to witness the scene of a suicide. I feared scarring them for life with the thoughts and images a suicide would produce. I concluded, by the grace of God, that I had hurt them enough already and it would prove selfish to kill myself. God broke through to my confused soul in that thought process. I couldn't put my babies through that tragedy, and I was afraid to break God's command not to commit murder. So with trembling hands, I unloaded the gun, cried myself to sleep again, and prayed things would be better in the morning.

My situation was complicated by a complete lack of knowledge. I didn't know what was wrong with me. I didn't know I had PMS—a hormonal condition that turned my life upside down. One night in my ignorance, I woke Buddy up and begged him to call our pastor and ask him to come right over. Buddy looked at the clock on our nightstand, saw that it was the middle of the night, and asked me "Why? What's wrong?"

I sat up in bed and cried, "Because I'm possessed and I need help!"

"You're not possessed," he said. "Honey, just go to sleep, and you'll be fine in the morning."

"No, I won't! Please call him!"

"What makes you think you're possessed?"

"Because I'm mad, and I just want to claw your eyes out, that's why!"

"Why are you mad at me?"

"I don't know!" I cried as I threw myself back on my pillow.

"Well, you're not possessed, and I'm not calling him."

I sat back up on the bed, with my arms folded across my chest, upset, shaking, and crying for absolutely no rational reason at all. Buddy moved over beside me, gently pulled me toward him, and held me until I calmed down. He didn't have any great words of wisdom or consolation; he just kept telling me he loved me, which was all I needed to hear. I didn't feel worthy of anybody's love—not Buddy's, not my children's, and certainly not God's. But Buddy loved me anyway. He was being Jesus with skin on at that moment—and so many more times that I could never count them. Imagine that— he loved me in spite of my sin. He loved me when I didn't love back. Buddy clearly saw my every weakness and loved me anyway. He offered unconditional love and tolerated my angry outbursts. He kept forgiving my words of attack and loved me anyway. I didn't deserve him or his love. In the arms of my husband, I finally grasped by experience what I had been taught my whole life about the love of God—it's unconditional! My goodness, my perfectionist qualities, my study of the Bible had all been sources of pride for me. Through the pain of PMS, a prideful young woman was finally exposed, and she was covered in the filthy rags of her own self-righteousness. I got a long, hard look at her, and I hated what I saw. But at the same time, I saw beside me a loving God who loved me despite my pitiful condition. He patiently waited for me to admit to my sinful pride and my sinful actions so he could begin the process of cleaning me up and removing those prideful roots I had fertilized for years. God used my husband's unconditional human love to guide me toward a new understanding of God's divine unconditional love.

> But we are all like an unclean thing, and all our righteousnesses are like filthy rags.
>
> Isaiah 64:6

Today, I know that without the grace of God, I am a hideous monster quite capable of attacking even those I love the most. Because of my own deliverance, I know there is hope for everyone when the grace of God is applied in their lives. When we perform good works in our own power, it looks like filthy rags to God. But when we recognize our own sinfulness and human limitations, we become beautiful material in the Master's hands and he can sew us into a fine tapestry fit for his own use and glory.

I understand what it's like to be so deep in a pit that you are not able to pull yourself up by your bootstraps or snap out of it. I tried and couldn't do it. I often worried that my chaotic ups and downs had ruined my children. I fretted that my angry and depressed behaviors had surely scarred them for life. I feared they would grow up to be serial killers taking revenge on the whole world because they had a crazy momma two weeks out of every month. Well, thanks to God, they turned out just fine. Not because of anything I did, but because God's grace is always sufficient. When I talk about those dark days, my kids do not seem to recall the same awful scenes that I do. Even Buddy reassures me, "Oh, you weren't so bad, really." But I know I was. It has taken me years to forgive myself, and I struggle to forget memories of spouting hateful words and being much too eager to spank rambunctious children. I know how much worse it could have been without God's intervention. I know where I could have been without the grace of God becoming a reality—not just a Bible lesson—in my life. My prideful spirit required brokenness before I could fully comprehend the application of grace in my own life.

> My sacrifice (the sacrifice acceptable) to God is a broken spirit; a broken and a contrite heart (broken down with sorrow for sin and humbly and thoroughly penitent), such, O God, You will not despise.
>
> Psalm 51:17 (AMP)

For the first time in my life, I had a broken spirit when I saw my sinful actions, and I repented for them. That's why I believe—and am so thankful—that God allowed me to endure horrible PMS for several years. Without that experience, I could easily have turned into the self-righteous church lady who looks down her nose at anyone who falls short of her version of godliness. But the experience of PMS caused the sinful nature that I had learned to hide so well to be brought to the surface and dealt with. In so doing, Mrs. Self-

Righteous learned that she wasn't one bit righteous outside the grace of God.

I was gradually educated on PMS and its devastating effects on women with the help of a young, sympathetic female gynecologist who diagnosed me with an extreme case of it. She recommended dietary changes, progesterone cream, and natural supplements that helped me to eventually curb the drastic mood swings I had suffered with for so long. But during the process of getting my PMS under control, it became a bit of a joke with the people who knew me well. I proudly wore my PMS badge and flashed it anytime I needed an excuse for my actions. My kids learned to run for cover in their rooms when I gave them sufficient warning by saying, "Mommy has PMS today." I wore PMS buttons and T-shirts to laugh at my condition. You've seen them, I'm sure. They carried slogans like "Beware! I'm armed and have PMS!" My next lesson was learning that no matter how whacky and out of balance my hormones were, it was never an excuse for sin.

Prior to PMS invading my life, I had been a prideful person consumed with outward appearances. I was proud that I didn't have "sin" in my life, proud that I was the "perfect" mom, proud that I was a "good" Christian. Doing the right thing just came easy for me. I was far from perfect, but the good things that I did were a result of my own strengths. I'm a firstborn, melancholy people-pleaser. I grew up with people expecting me to do the good and right things in life. So the goal of my life was to be a good girl and keep everyone happy by doing right both in the church and in the community. I was quite capable of excelling in this area, and anyone watching from the outside would have seen a good girl doing good works. Only after PMS invaded my life did I realize that it didn't matter what other people saw in me as much as it mattered what God saw in me. People can only see the outward actions, but God can see the inward motivations!

But if anyone builds upon the Foundation, whether it be with gold, silver, precious stones, wood, hay, straw, the work of each (one) will become (plainly, openly) known (shown for what it is); for the day (of Christ) will disclose and declare it, because it will be revealed with fire, and the fire will test and critically appraise the character and worth of the work each person has done.

1 Corinthians 3:12–13 (AMP)

God saw the motives in my heart. The good things I did were based on a motive to please people and do what was expected of me. However good those deeds may have been, one day they will burn up like dry straw on a windy day because I did them in my own strength and for the wrong motives. Thank God PMS came into my life to reveal to me that I was building on the wrong foundation—my own strengths and good works. I realize now that nothing good dwells in me unless the grace of God has put it there!

Indeed, PMS showed up and shattered my perfect little world. I had no patience for my little children, who expressed their energy with running, giggling, and screaming escapades that rattled every last frazzled nerve I had. It's funny to me now that I had worked so hard to teach my babies to walk and talk and then I just wanted them to sit down and shut up. One day I spanked Janie when she dropped her fork from her high chair. She didn't throw her fork in a tantrum; she just plain dropped it. I yanked her up out of her high chair, exposed her chubby little thighs, spanked them, then sat her back down and cried the rest of the day for being so harsh.

Episodes like this haunted my nighttimes as I relived every scene and wished I could undo them. I came to know what Jesus meant when he taught about the pride of the Pharisees. In Matthew 23:27, Jesus compares their pride to "whitewashed tombs which indeed appear beautiful outwardly, but inside are full of dead men's bones and all uncleanness." That description fit me to a tee when PMS dominated my life. I never fell into gross sin—as the world would define it—during this time, but my sin was gross to me. I was an emotional basket case and harsh to my family while at the same time I was trying to be a good person with a smile on my face outside the four walls of my little dollhouse. I had a scary monster living inside me, and PMS brought me face-to-face with her.

It finally became too hard to be good anymore; I just couldn't muster up the strength to do it. I didn't feel like being nice to Buddy or the kids. I wanted to do right, but it was beyond my ability to do it. I didn't want to be selfish, but I was. My sin nature floated to the surface just like scum on a stagnant pond, and I was repulsed at what I saw. Before PMS, I had fooled myself into thinking Romans 7 didn't apply to anyone who tried hard enough to be good and obey the Lord. Ha! What a joke of a Christian I was, bound by my own ignorance.

> For what I am doing, I do not understand. For what I will to do, that I do not practice; but what I hate, that I do. But now, it is no longer I who do it, but sin that dwells in me. For I know that in me (that is, in my flesh) nothing good dwells; for to will is present with me, but how to perform what is good I do not find. For the good that I will to do, I do not do; but the evil I will not to do, that I practice. O wretched man that I am! Who will deliver me from this body of death? I thank God—through Jesus Christ our Lord! So then, with the mind I myself serve the law of God, but with the flesh the law of sin.
>
> Romans 7:15, 17–19, 24–25

Today I now know that no matter how good I act, I am a sinner in desperate need of the grace of God to get through every minute of every day. Any good that I do is only by his grace, and I cannot take any credit for it in my own flesh.

Why would I be thankful for this experience and the torment I put my young family through? I'm most thankful because my gracious God has redeemed all the pain and frustration of it for his glory and our ultimate good. Not only did this trial illuminate the truth of Scripture to me, but it also provided an opportunity for me to help and comfort other young moms who also live in the pits of PMS.

Blessed be the God and Father of our Lord Jesus Christ, the
Father of mercies, and God of all comfort, who comforts us in all
our tribulation, that we may be able to comfort those who are in
any trouble, with the comfort with which we ourselves are com-
forted by God.

2 Corinthians 1:3–4

I've witnessed this verse in action through my PMS experience. A
spiritually intuitive friend had the compassion to call me and sug-
gest I might be suffering from PMS. As she explained the syndrome
to me, I was stunned to hear her describe my exact emotions. I was
even shocked as she shared her own PMS story with me. Here was
the most "have it all together Christian woman" I had ever met, and
she had already walked a mile in my shoes! To tell you the truth, I felt
exhilarated and liberated to know she understood. The best thing she
said to me that Sunday afternoon on the phone was, "Nothing you
can say will shock me." Her phone call set me on the path to healing.
Now I had a name for what ailed me, and I had a friend who didn't
think I was evil or crazy. She also recommended a women's health
center, where I found the doctor who helped me regain my sanity.

Years later as the Lord finally helped me put myself back
together, I began teaching and speaking at my church to both wom-
en's groups and a MOPS (mothers of preschoolers) program. It was
during one of those events that a young mother approached me after
the meeting with big, tear-filled eyes and said, "Thank you so much
for sharing your story. I've been going through the same thing, and I
just thought I was a bad mom." At that moment, I knew God had a
purpose for my trial, and if it helped just one mommy, then my pain
had been worth it. But the comfort I received has even hit closer to
home, as I've even been able to comfort my own grown daughter and
help her avoid the severity of PMS with preventative measures. I am
indeed thankful for both the comfort I've received and the comfort
God has allowed me to give.

I'm thankful for PMS because it taught me to war against my
flesh with the power of God. When I felt like saying something

hateful, I had to learn to bite my tongue. When I wanted to pout, run away, slam a kitchen cabinet, or lay across my bed—making a mountain out of a molehill—instead I forced myself to apologize. These were not easy battles, but I learned that the more you whip your own flesh, the less it acts up. Or perhaps a better way to phrase it would be, I learned to stop feeding my flesh, so it wasn't nourished enough to fight back with as much strength. This battle with my flesh will continue until my body is laid in its grave, but until that day, I'll pray for God's strength and grace to wage a successful war against it.

I'm thankful for the clarity my dreadful PMS experience revealed to my pious, church-lady mind. I looked at my own righteousness and saw the same filthy rags that God saw. I understand the concept of the grace of God, and my desperate need for it, after seeing my ugly inner self. I'm thankful God dealt with me, and even though I didn't pray the prayer below, he answered for me what David prayed for himself. When I wasn't smart enough or spiritual enough to pray this prayer, my merciful Father, ever full of grace, answered it for me.

> Lord, make me to know my end, and what is the measure of my days, that I may know how frail I am.
>
> Psalm 39:4

You may be curious about how I physically overcame severe PMS. I can tell you that it was once again the almighty grace of God as he led me to informative people and literature. The condition did not succumb overnight but rather, took years of implementing changes in my diet, reducing stress, and giving my body the supplements it required. As you will see in the following chapters, the sovereign hand of God was at work, as this new knowledge would become an integral piece in the puzzle of my life. I was learning vital information on natural ways to help the body heal that would prove crucial in the future for the very life of a loved one.

Without going through my experience with hormonal imbalance, I would not be the woman I am today—a woman who knows what she is apart from the grace of God. I'm a woman who knows that she is nothing without the Lord and that anything good *about* her is a result of his work *in* her. I'm a woman who cannot cast stones at another and who sees a woman in trouble and knows, "There, but for the grace of God, go I." How thankful I am that the awesome God cared enough to change me even if he had to use a difficult ordeal to accomplish the mission.

TRIAL FIVE: "AM I A HYPOCHONDRIAC OR JUST PLAIN NUTS?"

"Honey, I'll send you to any specialist you want to go see, but I can't find anything wrong with you. As far as I can tell, you probably have chronic fatigue syndrome." My doctor had exhausted all the resources available to him trying to find a source for all my physical complaints. He had ordered multiple tests and even asked me if I wanted him to check for HIV.

"I'm a highly unlikely candidate," I told him, "but at this point just tell me I have something so I know I'm not a nut or a hypochondriac!"

Every single test, even the MRI, was negative. So when my doctor kindly offered to send me to another doctor, I sighed and responded, "No, thank you." I thanked him for all his concern and efforts, and I walked out of his office disappointed but determined to try another avenue.

My symptoms had been going on vaguely for years—and intensely for the last few months. I was so tired some days I could barely function. Even shampooing my extremely short hair required resting my arms two or three times before I could finish. I often ran a low-grade fever, and I usually had a mysterious ache or pain somewhere in my body. Several times I stumbled or fell because my legs felt like spaghetti and just couldn't hold me up. I also developed a corneal condition at this time that baffled three different ophthalmologists. Only in my early thirties, my body felt ancient and uncooperative to me. My plumbing—if you know what I mean—no longer worked like it should. All these things began to take an emotional toll, and I fell into a slight state of depression. I had hoped my doctor would be able to pinpoint the root of my distress and fix it. He could not.

That's why I left my doctor's office determined to do something else. Modern medicine—as wonderful as it can be—was failing me on this particular issue. I had to take matters into my own hands to dig myself out of the pit I was in. I was sick and tired of being sick and tired. I drove across town and walked into an herbal shop that had recently opened. The gentleman who owned the store explained muscle testing to me and proceeded to test me for weak areas in my physical body. I left there with a sack full of dark bottles, a big subtraction in my checkbook balance, and high hopes that one of these herbal concoctions might help.

Buddy was a bit skeptical when he looked at the pile of pills I laid out to take with my supper, but he was willing to let me try anything if it made me feel better. Much to his surprise, in about ten days, I did begin to feel better. My mood was lifted, my energy improved, and I felt stronger. I was on the right track! I was nowhere near cured, but I had seen enough improvement to pay the herb man more money for more herbs.

My curiosity with natural and alternative methods began during my PMS trial, and then it turned into a full-blown obsession after I was diagnosed with chronic fatigue syndrome. I couldn't get my hands on enough literature to satisfy my hunger to know more about alternative and natural means to help the physical body. I read books and magazine articles on the subject and even pored over sales catalogs, reading what different supplements and herbs were used for. I discovered an informative cable television program on natural health, and once the Internet arrived at our house, I thought I had hit the jackpot on natural information! I experimented with different herbs, vitamins, and diet restrictions until I finally began to feel like my old self again. In fact, I think I actually felt better than my old self.

Today, I know that my physical ailments were complicated and perhaps caused by undiagnosed celiac disease, hypothyroidism, and the Epstein-Barr virus. Daily, I still have to guard my health, my stress level, and my diet to keep chronic fatigue from rearing its ugly head. If I stray too far from my health plan, I begin feeling symptoms again.

In my heart, I believe one of the reasons that God guided me to knowledge of natural health is so that I can manage these conditions. But you will read in an upcoming chapter another reason why it was so important for me to have this new knowledge of natural healing and access to alternative healing resources. On the darkest day of my life, this knowledge would play a critical role in preventing a loved one from perishing. You'll soon understand why I'm so thankful for this trial.

Some people might question why I didn't just ask God for healing and stand on faith to receive it. Let me answer that very question. First of all, I did pray for healing—a lot. God did not grant an answer to my prayer with a sudden and miraculous change in my body. Instead, he answered it in the way he deemed best. The Bible is full of promises, and many of them concern healing. In my situation, I learned that sometimes God gives a promise, but we have to fight to possess it. Let's look at an example from God's Word.

God promised the children of Israel the land of Canaan—the promised land. At their first opportunity to possess it, they were afraid of the giants in the land, so instead of getting to live in the promised land of milk and honey, they got to wander in the desert for forty years. At the end of their desert wandering, Moses died and God told Joshua to lead the people.

> Moses My servant is dead. Now therefore, arise, go over this Jordan, you and all this people, to the land which I am giving to them—the children of Israel. Every place that the sole of your foot will tread upon I have given you, as I said to Moses.
>
> Joshua 1:2–3

God promised to give the land to his people. Joshua led the people as they supernaturally crossed over the Jordan River. The promised land was already inhabited with people, some of whom lived in fortified walled cities. Jericho was one such city. God's plan for his people regarding the city of Jericho required some trumpet blowing, marching, and finally some shouting—and the walls of the great city fell down flat! Not a single arrow was shot or a single punch thrown. Just marching and shouting. That was an easy battle and the one we all recall from Sunday school. But the land was full of people in other cities that had to be conquered, and those battles—the ones we aren't as familiar with—required faith and mighty men of valor who prevailed in some bloody battles. The men did the hand-to-hand combat, but it was ultimately God who gave the victory and eventually gave them the land.

> So the Lord gave to Israel all the land of which He had sworn to give to their fathers, and they took possession of it and dwelt in it. The Lord gave them rest all around, according to all that He had sworn to their fathers. And not a man of all their enemies stood

against them; the Lord delivered all their enemies into their hand. Not a word failed of any good thing which the Lord had spoken to the house of Israel. All came to pass.

Joshua 21:43–45

The point I'm trying to make is this. Sometimes God's promises are handed to us on a silver platter, like the famous battle of Jericho. It was a victorious time, the people shouted praise to God for the quick way he conquered the city, and the whole region heard the testimony. But there are other times when God's promises are not handed over so quickly and we have to watch them work out slowly in our lives. It's in those times that God wants us working with him to the end result, as did Joshua and his army in the many other battles they fought. These are times when ground is gained a little at a time—and seldom noticed by the casual observer. We aren't able to raise our hands and give a fantastic praise report at church because the progress is so slow it almost goes unnoticed. Slow progress, yes, but praise God it's steady, and God is working no less than when he makes the walls of a city fall down with a shout. It is after we've seen victory in those bloody battles, which may have taken years to fight, that we understand why God told Joshua three times in Joshua chapter one to be strong.

Be strong and of good courage; do not be afraid, nor be dismayed, for the Lord your God is with you wherever you go.

Joshua 1:9

My battle with chronic fatigue and other health issues remains a fight for possession, and I often need reminded to be strong. The battle is still on going, and most people will never see it. I didn't get a miraculous healing in the fashion of the battle of Jericho. But I am not dismayed because my battle requires attention every day to proper care and feeding of both my body and my spirit. When I miss the mark—and believe me I do, especially when the smell of chocolate wafts through the air—I pay a price for it. I've had to

lean on God's grace and ask him for strength to avoid sugary temp-
tations that I know will ruin both my mood and my energy level.
The constant companionship of the Lord is a superior answer to
my prayer for immediate healing. I'm so thankful for a loving Father
who knows how to best answer my prayers when I cry out in need
to him.

TRIAL SIX: GIVING GOD MY CHILDREN

Now it came to pass after these things that God tested Abraham, and said to him, "Abraham!" And he said, "Here I am." And He said, "Take now your son, your only son Isaac, whom you love, and go to the land of Moriah, and offer him there as a burnt offering on one of the mountains of which I shall tell you."

Genesis 22:1–2

"You need to take your daughter home and sit her on the pot. There's nothing else wrong with her." I was mortified to hear those stern and condescending words come out of the mouth of the young intern doctor working in our local emergency room. My momma instinct knew that Janie was not constipated and that something else was seriously wrong. I asked the doctor to please call our family doctor since Janie had seen him two days before for the same complaint and she was worse on this late summer night, which was why we went to the emergency room. The doctor arrogantly repeated his diagnosis of constipation and refused to call our doctor. I was more than mad, but my own momma had brought me up to be respectful and never make a scene, so I didn't know what else to do but leave. I helped Janie off the hospital bed, and she leaned on me as we met Buddy in the waiting room.

"What did the doctor say?" he asked. When I told him the doctor's diagnosis, Buddy sighed and looked relieved, until he got a closer look at my face.

"She's not constipated!" I said through pursed lips. "Don't you think that's the first thing I checked as her mother? Let's get out of here!"

Janie could barely walk, so, looking quite bewildered, poor Buddy scooped her up in his arms and carried her to the car.

Janie was only eleven years old and was small for her age. She had lost weight in the last week since the pain in her side had now affected her appetite. Our family doctor suspected appendicitis at first, but her blood tests were all normal. He wanted us back in his office if she didn't improve. The only problem was that it was now the weekend and we couldn't get past the know-it-all intern in the emergency room. We put Janie to bed and decided to wait until Monday morning, when our doctor could see her again.

Buddy and I held each other in our bed and conversed about Janie's condition. She had developed dark circles under her eyes, and the color was draining from her face due to the continual pain. She had no interest in her usual activities and just lay on her bed holding her tummy. She had looked forward to watching the gymnastic events in the Summer Olympics on television, and the pain was so intense she couldn't even stay focused to watch it. She was always a tough little girl with a high pain tolerance, so when she complained, we knew it was severe. So that night, Buddy and I discussed what parents never want to discuss: What if it's something fatal? What if we lose her? We're not overly dramatic people who make mountains out of molehills, but we were scared. Our Janie looked so sick and frail, and medication did not ease her pain.

On that late night, I buried my head in Buddy's chest and asked him, "Can you give her to God?" He knew what I meant. I thought I could if I was forced to, but I wasn't sure he could lose his little girl and have his faith survive the loss.

My husband's voice never sounded as sweet and comforting as when he said, "Nothing could make me turn away from God—even losing her. Yes, I can give her to him."

Holding each other tight, with silent sobs, we quietly prayed together that night and begged God to heal our daughter—yet promised to love him even if he didn't.

Monday morning found Janie feeling more pain in her side, even after a good visit to the potty that nullified the emergency room doctor's diagnosis. Our family doctor saw Janie that morning and immediately ordered an ultrasound. While Janie and I sat in the radiology waiting room, a friend walked by, and with just a quick glance at Janie, she stopped and gasped. "Oh, my gosh!" "What's wrong with her?" she asked. Janie's pale face and weary, sunken eyes bore the signs of someone in relentless pain.

The ultrasound revealed that Janie had an ovarian cyst that was leaking fluid. The doctor waited two more days, hoping the condition would remedy itself—as they usually do. Janie was the exception, and she got worse over the next two days. The doctor made the compassionate decision to operate on the cyst and remove her appendix also. One look at Janie after the surgery told us she was fine. Her little freckles once again had a pink-toned background, and when she woke up, the sparkle had returned to her big, blue eyes. Janie was going to be fine, and so were her daddy and mommy because they had learned who Janie really belonged to—and it wasn't them. We didn't love our daughter one iota less, but we learned to let her go, a lesson every parent must learn to some degree with every child.

Three years later, our lesson was repeated more intensely with our son, Andy. He was eighteen when his eyelid began to swell and droop down, covering most of his eye. I called my former employer and friend who was an optometrist. He told me what I already knew—this was not a vision problem and I needed to get Andy to a neurologist. Andy had experienced a few brief episodes of this same condition since he was fourteen, and ophthalmologists were never able to find a source of the problem, which always resolved itself in a few days. This time, however, the swelling and drooping were worse and he was experiencing double vision.

I discovered that getting in to see a neurologist was much different than seeing your family doctor. We had to wait several days for Andy's appointment, and once again, the doctor was baffled. He ordered multiple tests, including a brain scan and a spinal tap. Then we had to wait, again, for those results. Meanwhile, Andy was getting worse. He was so dizzy he couldn't raise his head off his pillow without becoming nauseated. By this time, his eye was crossing, and we were all scared. We anxiously returned to the neurologist for the test results, only to hear those familiar words: "I can't find anything wrong. I don't know what is causing this." We were referred to an ophthalmologic-neurologist in Oklahoma City, which was another three-week wait. The wait was agonizing and tortuous for parents fearing that every day Andy went undiagnosed was one day closer to possible tragedy.

Once more, Buddy and I found ourselves clinging to each other late one night, discussing the unthinkable. We had been through a similar scenario with Janie, but this time while waiting for a diagnosis, we learned that Andy's symptoms were the symptoms of a brain tumor. Even though the brain scan was negative, we couldn't overlook the possibility that Andy could have a life-threatening condition—especially when we saw one of his eyes swollen, drooped, and now crossed and his other eye full of fear and uncertainty. We had to face facts, and we didn't like the facts we faced. Buddy and I were both active in our church and loved the Lord. That night, lying in bed, we questioned whether we could continue serving God if he allowed our boy to die. We shared our feelings, and through tears, we came to a mutual conclusion and whispered a prayer together: "Lord, we give our boy to you. We ask you to heal him in the name of Jesus. But we recognize your sovereignty, and if you choose to let our boy die, we pledge to not only continue serving you, but to love and praise you even in our pain. We give Andy to you and trust you to walk us through each day—no matter what it brings."

Every day we kept praying for Andy's healing. We also resisted the devil and rebuked him in the name of Jesus. Waiting to see the specialist in Oklahoma City was a long wait and a test of our patience. Finally, the appointment day arrived, and I anxiously drove Andy the three hours to the city to meet the doctor that we hoped could finally help him.

The doctor entered the exam room, and I immediately felt at peace when he introduced himself to us. His office was decorated with tasteful plaques that testified of his Christian faith. I silently thanked God for sending us to a skilled, Christian physician. He examined Andy's eyes and after a few minutes, turned in his chair toward me, winked, smiled, and said words I'll never forget: "Not to worry, Momma."

The good doctor finished looking into Andy's eyes and then gave us the "good news, bad news" diagnosis. "The good news is this won't kill him. The bad news is he'll have this condition the rest of his life." Praise God! I was so relieved that our son was going to be okay! I looked at Andy and saw the faint smile of relief on his face as well. Andy had a condition called pseudo-orbital tumor, which is an inflammation of the tissue surrounding his eye and not actually a tumor. But the inflammatory condition mimics the symptoms of a brain tumor. Andy was prescribed a high dose of prednisone to bring down the swelling, which was the only treatment for this condition that had no cure.

I knew that taking steroids long term would have negative effects, so I asked the doctor how he felt about me trying herbal treatments along with his prescription. I heard music to my ears when this Christian doctor endorsed my thoughts and said, "I say, go for it!"

The prescription quickly brought Andy's eyes back to normal, but it required six months to wean him down to a low dose of the prednisone. Simultaneously, Andy took herbs known for their anti-inflammatory properties, and I advised him on dietary changes since

I was unable to control what my grown son ate when he was away from home. When Andy saw the doctor for a six-month check up, the doctor said, "What do you say we live by faith for a while? Let's stop the medication." We rejoiced at hearing such a good report. Since that day in 1999, Andy has not had a severe flare up of this condition or needed prescription steroids to treat it.

We give thanks to God for his mercy to us when both of our children were in a health crisis. Of course, we're thankful that both of them are with us and healthy today. But when I reflect on those times, I'm also thankful for what God did in our hearts as their parents. God developed in us an attitude of sacrifice. We didn't want to give up our son or daughter, but if our sovereign Lord allowed that heartbreak to come, we would give them both to him and trust him with what we couldn't understand.

I have another reason to be thankful for these events. In both times, I had to speak up or go against popular opinion to follow what I believed God was leading me to do. In Janie's case, it was not accepting a qualified emergency doctor's diagnosis and trusting the mother's instinct God gave me instead. In Andy's case, it was treating Andy with dietary changes along with herbal and vitamin supplements. I had the blessing of Andy's doctor but the scrutiny and criticism of many others—including loved ones. How difficult it is when a person knows in her heart that God is leading in a certain direction, and she is surrounded by naysayers who have opposite opinions about what she should do. I had to overlook the comments and lifted eyebrows from those who doubted and stand on what I believed God had told me to do. Within six months, Andy's condition had reversed. Of course, God gets complete glory for that reversal, but I believe he can use any means he chooses to bring healing, including natural means. Andy's diagnosis led me to further interest in natural healing, and there is still another piece of the puzzle coming to reveal how crucial it was for me to have this knowledge. God is ever faithful. If God has given you a promise, a plan, or a job to do, no matter what people around you may say, I encourage you to listen for the voice of God, and when you know you've heard it, keep your feet planted firmly until you see the outcome God has promised you!

By no means do I dare compare myself with the father of our faith, but I can see a few minute similarities between God's testing of Abraham in regard to the command to offer his son, Isaac, and the stories I've just related here. Abraham, like any parent would, likely cringed at the words spoken to him when God tested his faith. But Abraham obeyed and proved his faith in God. Abraham was tested to the point that he actually held the knife in his shaking hand, dreadfully preparing to offer his son according to the Lord's command. God intervened and provided a substitute offering. What I find most fascinating in this story is what Abraham told his servants who had traveled with him and Isaac to the mountain where the sacrifice was to be made.

> And Abraham said to his young men, "Stay here with the donkey; the lad and I will go yonder and worship, and we will come back to you."
>
> Genesis 22:5

Abraham told his servants, "We will come back to you." Hebrews 11:17–19 points out that Abraham was prepared to offer his son in death but fully expected God to resurrect that boy to fulfill the promise of making Abraham a great nation through Isaac's descendants. No wonder he is called a father of the faith! Now read the blessing pronounced on Abraham and why it was given.

> Then the Angel of the Lord called to Abraham a second time out of heaven, and said: "By Myself I have sworn, says the Lord, because you have done this thing, and have not withheld your son, your only son, in blessing I will bless you, and in multiplying I will multiply your descendants as the stars of the heaven and as the sand which is on the seashore; and your descendants shall possess the gate of their enemies. In your seed all the nations of the earth shall be blessed, because you have obeyed My voice."
>
> Genesis 22:15–18

I pray that not a single reader will misunderstand what I'm about to comment on and that all will hear with a heart to hear and not reject it because of pain they may have endured in losing a child. I believe God gives us our children, and it's absolutely one of his most precious gifts to us. As much as we love our children, however, they should never come before him. God's well of love in our hearts is deep enough to love him foremost and still have more than enough love remaining for our spouses and dozens of children. But no one—not a spouse and not a child—should ever take the place in your heart that is reserved for God alone. God is not mean or harsh, and he doesn't take away a child from a parent who loves too much. But God desires first place in the lives of his people. God tested my husband and me when we made decisions to hand our children over to him—not out of fear, but out of love and trust. We were brought to a place of sacrifice where we were made willing to offer our children to our heavenly Father—who loved them even more than we were capable of—with a promise to praise him no matter what. This is not easy for me to explain, and I cringe at the thought of a parent who has actually lost a child to death, not understanding what I'm trying to say. I pray God ministers to those who have had to walk this path and that they would know how much the heart of God longs to love them and help them through their pain. I believe that in our case, God wanted to show us that as precious as our children are to us—and to him—he must be preeminent in our lives and we must trust him even in the most difficult of trials.

We gave our children to God. I believe this test was critical for me especially because I learned that the kids were not ours, but God's to control and use. Our job was to love them, train them, introduce them to God, and let him lead them from there. As a person with an inborn trait to control, this was a vital lesson for me for the sake of my children. Without this lesson of letting go, I could have turned into the mother who refuses to keep her nose out of her grown children's daily decisions. Instead, Buddy and I raised children who became independent and ultimately, after walking a few avenues of their own choosing, chose to dedicate their lives to the living God. If their daddy and I had not been tested to let them go, I could have easily smothered them with too much control and pushed them away from the very God I wanted them to love. Again, this is where we trust the omnipotent Lord who knows us—and our weaknesses—much better than we do and who is able to bring us to a crisis that will conform us more into his likeness. What an awesome God he is and so deserving of my thankfulness.

TRIAL SEVEN: ANOTHER DAY, ANOTHER JOB

Wives, in the same way be submissive to your husbands...like Sarah, who obeyed Abraham and called him her master. You are her daughters if you do what is right and do not give way to fear.

1 Peter 3:1, 6 (NIV)

I attended many Christian women's retreats where I was schooled in the finer points of submitting to my husband. Submission did not come naturally for me, but I gradually—and often quite reluctantly—learned to submit to my husband. I began my journey in submission by allowing my husband to lead me in the little things, like what time we should leave the house and how conflicts at our children's school should be handled. I toddled along in this area, struggling to give up control I felt I was born to have, and eventually I found freedom in letting my husband do what God created him to do: be the head of our family. My stress level decreased, and

I found peace when I learned that his shoulders were more capable of bearing the weight of decisions than mine were. I thought I had arrived at the peak of the submission mountain, until Buddy's job ended due to a plant closure. My aptitude to submit would face its biggest challenge.

Buddy had been a faithful employee at the Carbide plant for nearly twenty years. The corporate owners made a decision to close the local plant, and with just a few days' notice, my husband and several other employees were out of work. While many of his coworkers faced the closure with doom and gloom, Buddy was excited to see what God had in store for him. I was *mostly* at peace with the situation, *mostly* believing that God would meet our needs.

Buddy signed up at the local unemployment office, but he didn't sit around the house waiting for a job to find him. Almost forty years old, he had no marketable skills but a great work ethic, honesty, and a fantastic network of people. Within six days of losing his job, Buddy had a job offer. He came home to talk it over with me.

Buddy excitedly gave me the description of this job offer. Everything I had ever learned about submission disappeared after I carefully listened to every detail before I responded with, "What? Are you nuts? We can't afford for you to take that job! It's thirty miles away, it's a dead-end job, and the benefits and pay are below what we're used to! I think you need to keep looking for a better job." I really thought he had lost his ever-lovin' mind wanting to take this job.

Buddy looked me square in the eye and tactfully said, "Look, there's not a big demand for people who know how to make carbide. I've prayed about it; I feel good about this job and think I should take it."

It took me a few minutes to process in my born-to-control mind what my spirit was screaming at me: submit to your husband! All the submission lessons returned to my memory, and I had to decide whether or not I would submit to my husband's desire—taking a job that I thought was the stupidest thing I'd ever heard of. We discussed the job again at supper, and I knew Buddy was convinced that God wanted him to take the job. Seeing and hearing the conviction he held about this job helped me to submit. I trusted Buddy, he had always provided for us, but more importantly, I trusted God to speak to my man. I reasoned that if God could write on the wall and speak to a pagan king, he could surely get through to my godly husband. So if God was leading Buddy to this particular job—which I saw as a really bad idea—then my submission was not to Buddy, but to God himself. I told Buddy that I would support his decision to take this job. However, I maintained the right to say "I told you so" if it didn't work out—and the next morning he accepted the offer.

Here's the miracle in this story. With God's favor, and in just five short years, Buddy advanced from a technician's job to the sales manager in one of Oklahoma's largest RV dealerships. Not only was Buddy working in a job he absolutely loved, but he was in a cleaner and safer environment than he had been in at the old carbide plant and his salary was an unexpected blessing. We never anticipated the path God set Buddy's work shoes on. Only God could have orchestrated the situation, and he did so in spite of Buddy's skeptical—and sarcastic—wife! I came so close to thwarting the plan of God by my resistance to that original job offer. I'm so thankful that I have learned—often the hard way—to trust God by submitting to my husband.

But wait—there's more! That story is just one of my learning-to-submit-through-job-crisis stories. Midway through Buddy's success in the RV business, he accepted a sales job at a car dealership. I had not worked outside the home for almost a year and was perfectly content and happy staying at home. I've always been a homebody, never bored at home, and proud of my Susie-homemaker label.

Buddy had been at the car dealership for about three months. Then out of the blue, he called me one morning to say that the RV dealership asked him to come back and he was going to quit his current job and return to RV sales. Whoa! I felt a minor shake in the earth beneath my feet but managed to remain steady.

Later that same day: Andy called me from Arizona, where he and his horse were spending two weeks of vacation, team roping. He was calling to let me know he had decided to quit his job and stay in Arizona, where he planned to make a living in team roping. Our twenty-one-year-old son was leaving a great-paying job to pursue a dream with absolutely no guarantee of income, no insurance, and—worst of all—he planned to live in a different time zone from his momma. I thought, *Hold on, sister; things will surely quit shaking in a moment!*

Later that same day: Our daughter, Janie, was a busy senior in high school. Like many teenage girls, she had spread herself way too thin between school, extracurricular activities, and her job. She had worked at our local fast-food drive-in since she was in the eighth grade, she was the captain of the cheerleading squad, and she was about to graduate from both high school and vocational training school, where she studied to be a hairstylist. She arrived home that evening, stormed in the front door, put her hands on her hips, and said, "Well, I've just quit my job!"

Okay, at this point, I think I did feel the earth move under my feet, and I don't mean like Carly Simon's song. Major reality had just hit me. Not one person in our family was going to get a paycheck next week, and I did not want to return to the workplace. How I managed to stay calm on this day still baffles my mind. God must have been holding me steady because the only thing that kept going through my mind was, *Don't panic. This is only a test!*

It was a test. God proved to me that he was faithful to provide without my intervention, manipulation, or control. I allowed God to lead all three of them, and I did not interfere in their decisions. *Wow! Who was I becoming?* I realized God was changing me because this was definitely not how I would have responded in the past. He was transforming me into a daughter of Sarah—in more ways than one. Actually, my mother's name is Sarah, but God wants to call me a daughter of Sarah, as in the wife of Abraham. The opening verse of this chapter speaks of Sarah obeying her husband, submitting to his decisions, and not giving in to fear. The *NIV Study Bible* commentary on this verse says, "Christian women become daughters of Sarah as they become like her in doing good and in not fearing any potential disaster, but trusting in God."

I must admit, it was a bit scary the day three members of my family quit their jobs. I had to keep casting my cares on God over and over, several times a day. But as I considered the potential financial crisis these decisions could have caused, panic never gripped me as it would have in the past. As it turned out, the whole event wasn't even a blip on the family financial radar. Not only did God meet all our needs and provide better jobs, but our financial situation actually improved. Only God could bring that to pass while he simultaneously honored my submission. What a God he is, and how thankful I am for his transforming touches!

TRIAL EIGHT: "MOMMA, I NEED HELP"

And not many days after, the younger son gathered all together, journeyed to a far country, and there wasted his possessions with prodigal living. And he arose and came to his father. But when he was still a great way off, his father saw him and had compassion, and ran and fell on his neck and kissed him. And the son said to him, "Father, I have sinned against heaven and in your sight, and am no longer worthy to be called you son."

Luke 15:13, 20–21

I believe we all have defining moments in our lives. These defining moments might include times when we are forced to make a gut-wrenching decision or when we surrender our control in some fashion or when we are enlightened to a life-changing truth in the Scripture. Perhaps one defining moment in Jesus' life was in the garden of Gethsemane when he struggled to surrender to his father's plan. He so wanted to do his father's will, yet the foreknowledge of what this great task would require of him physically, emotionally, and spiritually was almost more than his flesh could bear.

> Then He said to them, "My soul is exceedingly sorrowful, even to death. Stay here and watch with Me." He went a little farther and fell on His face, and prayed, saying, "O My Father, if it is possible, let this cup pass from Me; nevertheless, not as I will, but as You will."
>
> Matthew 26:38–39

Jesus was faced with the decision of whether or not he would continue forward to the most difficult part of his earthly assignment: bearing the sin of the world and facing crucifixion. Can you imagine Jesus, the sinless Son of God, having all the sin of the world put upon him and bearing its punishment? No wonder Jesus dreaded this event. He seems to be asking his Father if there's any other way to accomplish his purpose without the fast-approaching pain, betrayal, and rejection he was about to meet. But even in the midst of his suffering, with love for mankind and a loyal heart to his Father, Jesus surrendered his will and asked for his Father's will to be done—no matter what it cost him personally. I call that a defining moment. I believe we all have these defining moments—obviously on a much smaller scale compared to Jesus' prayer in the garden of Gethsemane—when we must choose whether to seek our own selfish desires or do what is ultimately best for someone else.

I'll share a defining moment in my life with you that I really didn't want to put in this book for fear of it being misunderstood. It's so deeply personal that I've only shared it with my closest confidants before writing it down. I pray that my written words can convey to you the depth of this inner struggle and the freedom I found in surrender that I knew would cost me dearly. I ask you to read about my defining moment without judgment until you've read the entire chapter.

One afternoon, I was sitting with a friend who had lost a loved one about two years prior to the time of our conversation. She and I had both just attended the funeral of a mutual friend, George, who had died after a long illness. George had lived a godly life in his later years, and in the days just after his home going and before his funeral, several of his friends came to know Jesus as Lord. I commented to my friend, "Isn't it so precious that souls were saved even in the tragedy of George's death?" She looked at me with a facial expression that caught me completely off guard. My mind raced as I thought to myself, *Did I just say something wrong? Shouldn't all Christians rejoice when people are saved, even if it's through someone's death?*

With a tone that rang of condemnation to my ears, she replied, "If you told me everyone in our county would be saved, I still wouldn't give up my loved one." I sat in stunned silence. I didn't know what to say. Who was I to judge her feelings? At that time, I had never lost anyone in my immediate family except one grandparent. My mind was tumultuous as I tried to understand and sympathize with her comment. She was my friend, and I felt compassion for her because her heart was still hurting. I wondered how I would respond if I'd been through her trauma and loss.

Several hours later, disturbing thoughts still dashed across my mind as I imagined losing one of my own children and wondered if I would change my opinion on being thankful for salvations that occurred because someone died. I asked God to help me sort out the truth in my thoughts and feelings and not let me have a pious, unsympathetic attitude toward my friend who had suffered such grief and loss. After prayer and soul searching, I finally came to a conclusion—and I really didn't want to reach the conclusion I came to—but deep within my spirit, I knew it was right. This conclusion gave me a sense of surrender and oddly enough, even an unusual peace. The conclusion was this: if God asked me to surrender my child so that a revival so big would break out causing everyone in our county to be saved, I could not say no. The love of God that he has shed abroad in my heart and his grace abounding in me would cause me to say yes, even though I would hate the very idea of sacrificing my child.

It was then that I thought of Jesus' prayer in the garden of Gethsemane and how torn he was between his own flesh and the deep desire to do his father's will so mankind could know salvation. The conclusion for me was seeing the big picture, which suddenly became crystal clear. Eternity is what really matters. There are people in my county who will spend that eternity in hell—forever! I wouldn't want anyone, not even an enemy, to suffer eternal separation from God. Keep in mind, as the Holy Spirit was helping me think this all through, I knew beyond a shadow of a doubt where both of my children would spend eternity. They were both saved and baptized, and I was confident in their security in Christ.

At home that evening, I battled a feeling of guilt over the conclusion I reached. Was I a bad mother? Did I love my children as much as other mothers loved theirs? What was wrong with me that I would willingly surrender my child if God asked me to? Who in their right mind would give up their child? But that is the point. That thought wasn't from my mind; it was from the mind of Christ. No loving parent on the face of this earth would surrender his or her child for the sake of others unless God himself gave the grace and love to do so. I believe this conclusion was put in my heart from God because it's absolutely abnormal to feel this way.

So my defining moment came that day when in my heart, I surrendered my children to the will of God for his glory, knowing full well the unbearable pain I could feel, yet knowing I could trust God to grant me all I needed to deal with whatever he allowed in my life. I understood that his glory and salvation of souls took precedence over my desires and comfort. In my mind, I only fathomed losing a child to death. Little did I know at the time, but there was more than one way I could lose a child.

> May God not find complaints in us anymore, but spiritual vitality—a readiness to face anything He brings our way...We are here to submit to His will so that He may work through us what He wants. Once we realize this, He will make us broken bread and poured-out wine with which to feed and nourish others.
>
> —Oswald Chambers

During this same time, another dear friend and I were sharing how we prayed over our teenage children. She told me about a prayer she prayed but said it required guts if I also chose to pray this prayer. My curiosity was piqued, and I asked her to tell me more. She told me that she prayed her children would never get away with anything. I thought, *Wow! That does take guts!* Her rationale was that it's better for teens to get caught early so that rebellious behavior would not go unpunished and would hopefully deter future sinful acts. I thought that made perfect sense because so many teens do test the waters with wrong actions, and when they aren't caught, they feel safe enough to wade out deeper into situations that could eventually drown them. I pondered whether I could really pray that prayer and sincerely want God to answer it. *Would it be worth it to exchange the public embarrassment I would face if my kids got caught doing something bad to hopefully stop them from continuing on the rebellion road?* With a bit of dread, some apprehension, and a whole lot of trust in God, I began praying that very prayer over my children through their teen years.

> Fast forward through busy, prayerful years as the time of raising my children neared its end.

It was a gorgeous June morning in my backyard, and I was in my element. Tending my flowerbeds was my passion. I loved to take an empty bed and watch it transform into a sea of blooming flowers. I held the water hose over my petunias and snapdragons while they drank up the water and I drank up the relaxing sunshine. I was thinking how relaxed I was for the first time in years. I had been able to quit my part-time job working at the church office the previous month, and I was enjoying being home without the stress of working. Finally, I didn't feel pressure to constantly be on the run between work and school events for the kids. Andy was grown and had left our little nest, and Janie was going to start her senior year in the fall. I was so thankful that I could be home during her busiest year and just enjoy it with her. Buddy was successful in his job, and God was prospering us. Life was good.

That was the scenario the day my prayer life changed. Out of nowhere—and much to my surprise—I heard the voice of God speak to me. It wasn't an audible voice. It wasn't a quiet whisper in my spirit. I'm not sure how to describe it, but there was absolutely no mistaking it to be the voice of God telling me, "You have one year."

Often in the Bible when someone had an encounter with God, the first words heard were "fear not!" I didn't hear those words, but I knew in my spirit not to be afraid. I felt a strange peace when I heard God say, "You have one year." I didn't have a clue what was coming, yet I knew deep within my spirit that in one year, life would be hard—really hard. I knew this, yet I still had confidence that God would walk me through the trouble that was on its way. My mind began to race with all the possible calamities that might come to me. Did this mean Buddy or one of the kids would die? With one teenager at home and a young adult living on his own, thoughts of unwed pregnancies came to my mind, even though neither one of them was in a relationship. I had fleeting thoughts that perhaps a national disaster was coming, but that didn't coincide with what I felt in my spirit. I knew that the trouble would be on a personal level in my family. I had to force myself to cast down those imaginations. Trust me, during that year I had to practice and train myself to cast down thoughts and imaginations as I constantly battled the anxious question of, "What's going to happen in one year?"

I'm a doer and a fixer, so I immediately began to prepare for my unknown event. I've always said, "If my house is in order, I can handle war. If it's a chaotic mess of clutter, I can't handle anything." So I started getting my house in order. I cleaned, I organized, and I purged clutter. I painted. I stayed on top of every chore and responsibility that I could. But most importantly, I prepared for my unknown event spiritually. I made a list of scriptural prayers, and I interceded daily for my family. I've always prayed over my family, but during this year of preparation, I prayed as I'd never prayed before. These were prayers for wisdom and prayers for protection for those in crisis. I also prepared for my event physically. I continued in my study of natural health and learned more ways to live a healthy lifestyle. I wanted to be armed and prepared on all fronts for this difficult thing God had warned me about. I shared with Buddy the words I heard from God, and I remained prayerfully focused on it the entire year.

Exactly one year from the day God spoke to my heart, the telephone rang. There was a problem in the church office, and I was asked to come and set the financial books in order. I didn't want to return to work, but this had to be done and I seemed to be the only person at the time equipped and available to do it. So I plunged myself into balancing the past nine months of financial records. This was not an easy task, and the stress was tremendous. Coming home one evening after a long day at work, Buddy said to me, "Well, now you know what God warned you about." He had remembered that it was time for the unknown event to occur.

Shaking my head, I replied, "No, I don't think this is it. I don't feel a release yet. There's something else coming." The stressful situation in the church office was the beginning of the most tumultuous time of my life, and I was thankful for the warning God gave me so that I could be prepared.

A few weeks went by, and my brain was fatigued with number crunching, as I was still buried in the financial records at church. Besides keeping up with the current workload, I had nine months of bank statements to reconcile and the matching financial reports to do over, as well as update other office records that had been neglected. My concentration was broken one day when the door chime rang, indicating someone had opened the main door. I pushed the chair back from my desk and headed into the long hall to meet whoever the visitor was. I was surprised to see my twenty-two-year-old son walking toward me. He was dressed in his work clothes, and it took me less than a moment to know something was terribly wrong for him to be here in the middle of the day. Walking toward him, the light from the entry door behind Andy created a shadow that prevented me from seeing his facial expression until I got within a few feet of him.

My pounding heart was quickly justified once I looked into his sorrowful eyes and asked him, "Honey, what's wrong?"

We went into the nearest room for privacy and sat down together. I leaned toward my own sweet flesh and blood who sat with his head hung low, and I watched him struggle to verbalize the anguish that was in his heart. In a matter of seconds, hundreds of scenarios played out in my mind, speculating what his dreaded news might be. Finally, he summoned the courage to speak, cleared his throat, raised his eyes to meet mine, and said, "Momma, I need help. I'm on drugs. Can I come home?"

I'm not sure what was most shocking to me, the upsetting news or my reaction to it. I didn't cry. I didn't scream. I didn't faint. I didn't shame Andy or get mad at him. I felt the blow of his confession with relief. Finally, I knew what I had spent a year of my life preparing for. This was what God had warned me about. I finally knew what the enemy was, and I was ready, willing, and anxious to run to the battle and fight for the life of my son. I knew it would be hard, but I knew that my Deliverer would walk me through the bloody war and bring victory—one way or another.

I don't want to give the impression that I'm a super saint. Believe me, I had my moments and I shook with fear more than once. But just like a warrior in battle, I didn't have time to think about myself or throw a pity party about the situation I faced. My kid was in trouble with a capital T! He was the priority right then, not me. There wasn't time to ask why or try to fix blame. It was time to suit up with the armor of God and fight. I was ready to face the devil himself to save my son from destruction. Perhaps for the first time in my life, I didn't consider myself in any fashion and I completely gave all of me—my time, my thoughts, my prayers, my money, and all my energy—for the sake of someone else. I wasn't a super-strong saint—just a momma super prepared by a gracious God!

Andy is an extremely private person, quite unlike his momma, who is an open book. I do not feel at liberty to tell his entire story; in fact, I'm pushing the family envelope to tell the story from my perspective only. What I do want to share about him is that he moved home immediately with a truly broken spirit, much like the prodigal son in Luke 15. Andy took full responsibility for his actions, never excusing himself or blaming anyone, and he submitted to everything his daddy and I asked of him in the process of getting him past his addiction.

The early days of Andy's homecoming were intense. I was completely ignorant of the drug he was addicted to, and I didn't have a clue what to expect or how to help him. For three long nights, I fiercely searched the Internet after my family went to bed, and in those late-night hours, God led me to the information I needed to help my boy. Andy quit his job, and we took care of his financial obligations for four months while we did our own in-house rehab. I feel it's important to note that we did not do a financial bailout here. I explained to Andy that he had one opportunity for financial help, and if he returned to his addiction, we would not help financially again. He also understood that he was to pay us back every penny, which he did. We didn't care about the money but felt that it was important for Andy to pay us back for his own sake and self-esteem.

During Andy's first few weeks back at home, I rarely let him out of my sight. He went to work with me and did odd jobs—for free—around the church. When we were home, I kept him busy with projects around our house. I believe this made him feel better about himself, and sweating in our Oklahoma heat was a good way to detoxify his body. I constantly reassured him of our love for him, and I prayed openly over him often. I implemented what I had learned about nutrition and supplements that both nourish and detoxify the body, and we all followed a strict diet along with Andy. Every morning in my quiet time with the Lord, I would ask for wisdom to know what to do spiritually to help my son. Each day God provided something. On some days he gave me an idea for a topic to discuss with Andy, some days he provided a Christian tape to listen to, and on other days, he instructed me to have Andy reach into his pained soul and write how he felt.

God led us to two doctors who helped Andy tremendously. One was a Texas nutritionist with a PhD, and the other was a local chiropractor. Both used alternative healing methods that were huge factors in Andy's deliverance. I'll forever be grateful to these two men who played such an important role in my boy's recovery.

We were blessed to be surrounded by supportive friends and family. While they were all heartsick with us, they provided Andy reassurance of their love, as he was silently desperate for that assurance. When Andy couldn't bear to look them in the eye, they all had their ways of reaching out to him. Some sent cards, some just came and hung out with him, others insisted on hugging his neck, and still others stayed on their knees in intercessory prayer. Each act of love and kindness is forever etched in my memory—and I'm sure in Andy's also—and I'm forever grateful to those who chose to be Jesus with skin on to my troubled boy.

The day Andy came home, his daddy looked at him through tear-filled eyes and with a quivering voice told him, "Son, you'll get through this, and when it's all over, you'll be a better man." Our personal drug war was full of hard-fought battles, but in the end, God was faithful and our boy was delivered. Today, I'm proud to watch my son grow and mature in his walk with the Lord. He took a walk on the dark side, returned home with the broken heart of a prodigal, and emerged a different—and better—man.

At this point in the story, I need to expound on two things from the background of this trial, the first being the act of surrendering a child for the sake of God's glory. Let me be perfectly clear that God did not lead my son down a path of drug use, but he was no less with him during the whole ordeal. I've wondered if Andy's experience was similar to Peter's sifting, which I wrote about in an earlier chapter. Did Satan ask to sift my son? How the sovereignty of God, the providence of God, and our own personal choices work hand in hand is beyond my understanding. No doubt, Satan's intent was destruction. Andy's own free will choices revealed his weaknesses. Yet through it all I believe God not only salvaged but *used* every sinful detail of Andy's prodigal years for his glory. Those who have observed the transformation of my son over the time he's been drug free cannot help but give God both credit and glory for the change. I believe that the days of God getting glory for Andy's testimony have only just begun. Deep in my heart, I know that someday his story will indeed lead to the salvation of souls as God uses it in mightier ways.

It is a difficult thing to surrender your child, even to a loving and faithful God. I discovered that God will grant the grace to do so and, when it's done, he gives a peace that does pass all understanding. Parents should place their children in God's capable hands and trust God to do his work in them, even if that includes a sifting at the hands of Satan. If this thought is too much for you, I wonder if you think Jesus loved Peter less than you love your child. Not likely, yet Jesus allowed Peter to be sifted. Even with our love and best intentions, we cannot compare the job we do *with* our children to the job God will do *in* them, however he chooses to go about it. He loves them more than we do, and he alone sees the dross deep in their souls that only he can purge out to bring them more into the likeness of his Son, Jesus. Surrendering a child is a good—and loving—thing to do.

I also believe that God was testing my heart the day I surrendered my son to him. We know that God tests our hearts—although remember, it's never to evil. God tested Abraham when he asked him to offer his son, Isaac. We know the story of how God provided a sacrifice to take Isaac's place and Abraham named the place Jehovah Jireh, "the Lord Will Provide" (Genesis 22:14). What I find interesting is that the definition of *Jireh* means so much more than "provide." It also has a definition of "sees." So it appears that Jehovah Jireh translates as the "God Who Sees and Provides." This makes me wonder if during the ordeal with Abraham and Isaac, God saw Abraham's heart, which was willing to sacrifice his own son for God, and then God provided the substitute. Of course, God already knew that Abraham would obey, and God provided a sacrifice before Abraham's hand ever held a knife over his son's body. Here's the point I'm trying to make: I believe God was testing my heart the day I surrendered my children, which was long before Andy chose to surrender himself to drugs. God knew how I would respond to that test, but I didn't. God didn't take my son down an evil road, but he knew my son was headed there. Because God knew my son's future, he graciously prepared my heart to handle the pain of a prodigal and have the reassurance that God was always in control. My surrender before any of this occurred prepared my heart—a mother's heart—to avoid the bitterness or despair it could have embraced when faced with the frightening facts of having a son in the grip of drug use. Without surrendering Andy, I may have shaken my fist in the face of God for letting our family face public shame. Had God not led me down a path of surrender, I may have faced the ordeal with a self-centered attitude, thinking only of how Andy's addiction affected me, and I would have been unable to focus on him and his pain. That kind of attitude would have prevented me from helping Andy at all. Had I not surrendered my boy, my own controlling grip on his life may have destroyed him in ways much more destructive than his drug abuse. Yes, I do believe my heart was tested when God dealt with me that afternoon. But Jehovah saw my heart, which by his grace was willing to surrender a most precious person in my life for his glory, and God provided deliverance. Oh, how thankful I am for all of it—the test, the seeing, and the provision.

Indeed, Jehovah Jirah provided me one year of intense inter-cession for my family. He provided the experience, knowledge, and connections to doctors and seasoned intercessors to bring healing to my son physically, emotionally, and spiritually. When I recall all the intricacies of this trial, the providing hand of Jehovah Jirah was everywhere! How sad when we go through trials and never take time to look closely for the many ways God provides in the midst of them.

The second thing I need to explain is my prayer that my kids wouldn't get away with anything. Andy certainly did get away with many things. As he has gotten older, he has shared and confessed some of his many shenanigans. I have learned that he indeed got away with much. However, when Andy hit the rock bottom that finally brought him to his senses, it was because he had been caught. Thankfully it was not a law enforcement situation, but a situation where he could no longer hide his sinful addiction. That was an answer to the prayer I'd prayed for several years. It shattered my blissful ignorance, but praise God; it brought an end to Andy's destructive behavior. Surely the prodigal's father in Luke 15 prayed for his son as well. I wonder if he asked God to do—or allow—whatever it took to bring his boy back to both his earthly and heavenly fathers. Do you have the guts to ask God not to let your kids get away with anything? Do you have the guts to ask God to allow whatever it takes to bring your prodigal home? God answered my prayers and brought my prodigal home, for which I'm eternally thankful.

> As the deer pants for the water brooks, so pants my soul for You, O God.
>
> Psalm 42:1

This trial with my son offered so many reasons to be thankful, as there were lessons to learn on many levels. One of the things I'm thankful for is how this changed my worship experience at church. We attended a church where lifting your hands in praise was common. That is something I've done all my life, but the first Sunday morning after Andy's return home found me worshiping like I'd never worshiped before. I was desperate to enter into the presence of God in corporate worship. This Sunday morning, with my husband on one side and my son on the other side, no power on earth could have kept me seated in the pew when the worship music began. I was desperate to praise God with a grateful heart for bringing my prodigal home. I was desperate to give God the glory for sparing us the pain that would have surely come had Andy not come to his senses when he did. I was desperate to receive what only God could supply in the middle of this family storm to prepare me for the uncertainties of what tomorrow would bring. I was desperate to ask God for wisdom and strength for my family to endure until the storm clouds parted. Never in my life had I found myself so thankful. My uplifted hands represented to me more than just a common Sunday-morning ritual. My lifted hands were a sign of surrender to my Lord, whom I trusted with the life of my son. My arms waved in gratitude to a God who never left my boy's side and orchestrated circumstances that brought him back to the safe haven of his home. With both my arms extended toward heaven, they also symbolized a funnel as I asked my Lord to fill me with himself. The tears dripped from my face, and I didn't care who saw or what they thought. My God and I were desperate for each other, and it was our moment to commune with one another. There was no pretense, no going through the motions, and no phoniness in my spirit that day—just my soul panting to be satisfied with God's presence just as a deer pants for satisfaction from the water brooks. When the worship service ended, I sat back down in my padded pew a new woman. Oh my, I never realized how true, unashamed worship could touch the very depth of my soul until that morning when I found myself entering into his gates with thanksgiving and into his courts with praise. I was thankful to him, and I blessed his holy name.

> Forgetting those things which are behind and reaching forward to those things which are ahead…
>
> Philippians 3:13

Another reason for thankfulness in this trial is how it taught me to have a new perspective on mercy. When my prodigal came home, one of my first thoughts was to drag every dirty detail about his entrance into this sin out of him so I could not only try to understand it but also get the county sheriff to arrest those responsible for promoting this destructive behavior. Those were fleeting thoughts, and I never acted on them. I suddenly saw in my mind other mothers' sons who were in trouble and needed grace and mercy in their lives, just like my own son. I went to Andy and said with all sincerity, "I do not need to know a single detail of your past unless you feel you need to talk about it. As far as I'm concerned it is all washed by the blood of Jesus and cast as far as the east is from the west. So let's do like the Bible says and forget those things which are behind us and go forward."

I must admit that this is completely opposed to my personality. As I just mentioned, my nature would be to get the whole picture and do all I could to stop this from happening to anyone else. But God did a gracious work in my own heart at that moment, and for the first time in my legalistic life, I had true compassion and mercy for drug addicts—whether it were my own flesh and blood or a stranger lying in a dark city alley. I felt with my new heart what God must feel when his children come to him. Their past doesn't matter, and he doesn't need to rehash the details of their sin. Just knowing they are repentant and have asked for forgiveness is sufficient. Of course, there will always be earthly consequences to our sins, but the heart of God—and this momma's changed heart—just wanted to reach forward to those things which were ahead. In my own pious life, I never felt a true need for mercy. But now my son stood in a place where without mercy, he had no future. My heart of stone was replaced that day with a heart of flesh, by the grace of God! How thankful I am for this new understanding that does not excuse any sinner but grasps how a loving God longs to extend mercy and forgiveness freely to the repentant heart and does not hold over his head those things which are behind.

And Saul said to David, "You are not able to go against this Philistine to fight with him; for you are but a youth, and he a man of war from his youth." But David said to Saul, "Your servant used to keep his father's sheep, and when a lion or a bear came and took a lamb out of the flock, I went out after it and struck it, and delivered the lamb from its mouth; and when it arose against me, I caught it by its beard, and struck and killed it. Your servant has killed both lion and bear; and this uncircumcised Philistine will be like one of them, seeing he has defied the armies of the living God." Moreover David said, "The Lord, who delivered me from the paw of the lion and from the paw of the bear, He will deliver me from the hand of this Philistine." And Saul said to David, "Go, and the Lord be with you!"

1 Samuel 17:33–37

Who doesn't love the story of young David and his confidence to face the warrior giant Goliath? The passage above explains where David got his gumption—from previous experience! The Lord had allowed young David to face killer beasts while shepherding sheep for his father. Because of those previous battles, David had confidence not only in his ability but in the delivering power of the Lord. Before David ever faced Goliath, God had prepared him with victories over the lion and the bear. When I look back over the trials in my life, I see how the sovereign hand of God prepared me to face this most difficult challenge with my son. If this trial had been my first taste of the battlefield, I would have surely lost the fight. But I'd already witnessed the faithfulness of God firsthand, and I was confident in his presence to equip me with every weapon I needed and then to lead, guide, and deliver the enemy into my hands!

> Now these were the numbers of the divisions that were equipped for the war, and came to David at Hebron... Of Zebulun there were fifty thousand who went out to battle, expert in war with all weapons of war, stouthearted men who could keep ranks... Of the Danites who could keep battle formation, twenty-eight thousand six hundred; of Asher, those who could go out to war, able to keep battle formation, forty thousand; of the Reubenites and the Gadites and the half-tribe of Manasseh, from the other side of the Jordan, one hundred and twenty thousand armed for battle with every kind of weapon of war. All these men of war, who could keep ranks, came to Hebron with a loyal heart.
>
> 1 Chronicles 12:23, 33, 35–38

Some time after David killed Goliath, David's army was assembled according to the word of the Lord. The scripture above lists the numbers and types of men in David's army. They are described as "expert in war." These soldiers were seasoned fighters with battlefield experience, which prepared them for the current war. Four times in this passage, certain groups of men were commended because they were able to keep ranks. I'm especially intrigued with this statement about their ranks because it indicates that they always stood their ground and didn't run away from the fight—they were mentally and spiritually prepared. They were also physically prepared because they were armed with every kind of weapon to fight their enemies. These soldiers with previous battle experience had been prepared and proven able to face the next foe confident and well armed.

As I look back over the trials I faced prior to the one I faced with my prodigal, I can see how the previous trials prepared me for victory in the one battle that most threatened my family. Oh, how thankful I am that God prepared me, or else I would have not been armed, not been expert in war, and I would have surely broken rank and ran at the first sign of attack. Had I not been acquainted with the battlefield already, this most important fight may have ended in tragic defeat. What gratitude I have to a loving heavenly Father who let my feet learn to keep ranks on the battlefield.

In the midst of this trial, I had faith in God, but I still couldn't be certain how it all would end. I knew that the statistics were against us, as relapse is high with the drug addiction Andy had. The one thing I did believe was that God was faithful. I hung on to a belief that even in a worst-case scenario, he would strengthen me. Sarah, Abraham's wife, was an example and inspiration to me. Her name is recorded in God's "Faith Hall of Fame" of Hebrews 11. God promised that she would bear a child in her old and barren body. In what was a hopeless situation to the natural eye, she judged God faithful. In my trial, there were days that I felt overwhelmed and apprehensive of the future, but I judged God faithful. Some days I felt surrounded by trouble, so I clung to the knowledge that my God was faithful. Some days I fretted over the ups and downs of my son's recovery process, and in the struggle of it, I kept reminding myself that God was faithful. When others didn't understand what we were going through and they criticized our approach, I begged God to remind me that he was always faithful. In the end, I can proclaim from the mountaintops that when the enemy came into my home like a flood, God indeed was faithful! This isn't a guess I have about him. This isn't something I've heard about him. This is something I know about him. He is forever faithful, and I know it!

There are times when there is no storm or crisis in our lives, and we do all that is humanly possible. But it is when a crisis arises that we instantly reveal upon whom we rely. If we have been learning to worship God and to place our trust in Him, the crisis will reveal that we can go to the point of breaking, yet without breaking our confidence in Him.

—Oswald Chambers

After this trial, I have more confidence in the faithfulness of God. Besides that, I also gained a better understanding of the merciful heart of the Father God for the prodigal. I'm thankful for his mercy, I'm thankful for his faithfulness, but I'm most grateful to just know him better. Without this trial, would I have known my Lord as well? Probably not. Would I like a do-over in life for my son so he could avoid the pain of his addiction? Absolutely. Would I exchange the people he and I have both become for the people we both were? Never. Through it all, I find more reasons to give thanks.

Blessed be the God and Father of our Lord Jesus Christ, the Father of mercies and God of all comfort, who comforts us in all our tribulation, that we may be able to comfort those who are in any trouble, with the comfort with which we ourselves are comforted by God.

2 Corinthians 1:3–4

Another reason I'm thankful for this trial is that it prepared me to minister to and comfort a loved one. He and I grew up together as children, until my family moved sixty miles away. While I sipped my coffee and watched the local news one morning several months into Andy's recovery, my heart nearly stopped when I heard my loved one's son's name. His mug shot on the television and the crime he was accused of were an immediate shock. I suddenly had such compassion for my loved one and his parental heart because I knew exactly how he felt! Although my son was never arrested, he did break the law in his addiction. I knew the heartache of a parent whose child had publicly failed. I knew from experience the gut-wrenching pain this father would feel if loved ones turned their backs on his son because they couldn't cope with the embarrassment of the boy's sin. I prayed and asked God to show me what I could do to minister to him and his family.

God led me to the computer, where I sent him a simple, encouraging e-mail. Besides sending my love and prayers, I briefly shared my own story so he would know I could relate to his broken heart due to the similarity in our situations. For the next few weeks, God would direct my words sent through e-mails and use me to help comfort a man who meant so much to me. If I could have erased the choices of our children, I certainly would have. But I could not, so I used my heartache as an opportunity to help. God had comforted me in my trial, and it equipped me to pass along that same comfort to another hurting heart in such desperate need of it. And for the opportunity to be used by God in sharing small pieces of comfort, I again find reason to be deeply thankful for my trial.

I feel compelled to give a word of encouragement to the person whose loved one is in crisis and shows no intent of making a change for the better. We need to make constant intercession for the person in trouble. That trouble I'm referring to could be anything from an addiction to a character flaw that God wants to remove from your loved one's life. Intercession is crucial, but, friend, be forewarned: it may make things temporarily worse. But that's a good thing. As is the case with tough love, your loved one may need to experience brokenness before he experiences healing. If healing is our goal, then I say, bring on the brokenness. On this very subject, Oswald Chambers warns us not to have emotional sympathy with them, but to stay identified with God's interest for our loved one.

> As we continue on in our intercession for others, we may find that our obedience to God in interceding is going to cost those for whom we intercede more than we ever thought. The danger in this is that we begin to intercede in sympathy with those whom God was gradually lifting up to a totally different level in direct answer to our prayers. Whenever we step back from our close identification with God's interest and concern for others and step into hav-

ing emotional sympathy with them, the vital connection with God is gone. We have then put our sympathy and concern for them in the way, and this is a deliberate rebuke to God.

—Oswald Chambers

In other words, we must intercede for God's best to be accomplished in those we love. They may need discomfort in their lives to push them to a place where they finally come to their senses. Sounds like the prodigal son story to me. It was the difficulty he faced that forced him to face himself and the sinful choices he had made before he would come to his senses and go home.

I've witnessed this in areas that have nothing to do with addictions, but with personality or character issues. If God is trying to break someone's spirit to purge out a sinful characteristic, then our sympathy will only enable them to stay where God does not want them to remain. This will be a hard concept for some to swallow. Let's look at two examples to help make this concept clearer.

I've never been to military boot camp, but we all know that it is not a pleasant walk in the park. Why isn't it? Shouldn't our military be nice to those men and women who voluntarily join to serve their country? Heavens no! If you really care about those servicemen and women, you will want them trained and conditioned so they can successfully face their missions. Part of the military training is breaking the spirit of these brave people. They have to learn that their wants and needs are secondary to what is best for all. They must change their thinking from "it's all about me" to "it's all about us." They must learn to follow orders without question. Once those spirits are broken, the rebuilding begins, and at the end of the training, a confident, disciplined soldier emerges who is willing to lay down his own life for his fellow soldier and his country.

Consider Peter and how he denied the Lord within a few short hours of saying he would follow Jesus anywhere—including to death. Peter was prideful and self-sufficient, like many of us are. Could God have protected Peter from the situations that caused Peter to deny Christ? Sure he could have! But Peter was a changed man after the brokenness he felt after his public denial of Jesus. In our limited vision, we might think that Peter's denial—even though he was sorry for it—nullified him from serving Christ in the future. Oh, but Jesus saw the bigger picture and the new and improved Peter.

> He said to him the third time, "Simon, son of Jonah, do you love Me?" Peter was grieved because He said to him the third time, "Do you love Me?" And he said to Him, "Lord, You know all things; You know that I love You." Jesus said to him, "Feed My sheep."
>
> John 21:17

Peter was transformed from an arrogant, prideful man to a man who realized he could do nothing without the power of God. That is the kind of man Jesus wanted to use, and use him he did! It was Peter—after a public denial and a public restoration by Jesus—who preached the first public sermon on the day of Pentecost, leading thousands to salvation.

> And with many other words he testified and exhorted them, saying, "Be saved from this perverse generation." Then those who gladly received his word were baptized; and that day about three thousand souls were added to them.
>
> Acts 2:40–41

Rather than leave Peter a prideful and self-sufficient man, Jesus allowed him to be broken so God could use him for kingdom growth. Keep this in mind when you think of your prodigal loved one. Intercede for them and trust God to allow whatever it takes to bring them to the brokenness that will lead to their healing. Meanwhile, stay out of God's way and do not enable your precious one to remain in a sinful condition by protecting them from the consequences of their actions—whether it's a drug addiction or an arrogant attitude.

> For our light affliction, which is but for a moment, is working for us a far more exceeding and eternal weight of glory.
>
> 2 Corinthians 4:17

Remember to be thankful for adversity in your life and in the life of your loved ones. God used adversity to push my prodigal—and his momma—to a higher level in him. And in the end, it's a story to be thankful for, as we've felt the transforming and restoring hand of our loving God.

> So I will restore to you the years that the swarming locust has eaten.
>
> Joel 2:25

TRIAL NINE: LEARNING CONTENTMENT AT HOME

But seek first the kingdom of God and His righteousness, and all these things shall be added to you.

Matthew 6:33

We've all heard that we should be content with what we have; we should give to God and trust him to meet all our needs. But preaching contentment is easier said than done. Contentment does not come naturally. Our flesh always wants more, bigger, and better, whether it's a piece of chocolate cake, a fashion accessory, a vehicle, or a house. Paul gives us insight into contentment in Philippians 4.

For I have learned in whatever state I am, to be content.

Philippians 4:11

Paul said he had learned to be content. Contentment must be learned, and how will we learn contentment if we always get the things we want? We won't. We would be self-centered, spoiled, and immature. I believe God wants to prosper his children so he can bless them more as they bless others. But I believe he will seldom do this before they learn to give, manage, appreciate, and be content with what he has given them. God doesn't want anything to come before our relationship with him, and often our quest for material goods will do just that. There is nothing sinful in having nice possessions. In fact, God delights in blessing his children. But God wants nothing—especially possessions—to take precedence in our minds over him. When we put God first in our thoughts and in our actions, it will cause us to learn the meaning of contentment. We will no longer have worry or concern about our possessions because he will make sure we have all that we need. It took a long time for me to learn contentment, and God used my homes to help teach me this valuable lesson.

Have you ever felt the walls closing in on you where you live? Even with an addition to the house, we were quickly outgrowing our little dollhouse. I constantly criticized the cramped quarters and lack of cabinet space. That was my first opportunity to learn the lesson of contentment, but I failed at being a good student in that subject. Years later, after finally learning my lesson, God provided an opportunity to practice what I'd learned. I'll admit it was a struggle, and I felt like a student retaking a test I'd passed before. After a quick refresher course, I found that the test was easier to pass the second time around. Here's my story.

We had tried off and on for years to sell our little dollhouse. There just never seemed to be a buyer. We had built on to our home when our daughter was born and later discovered we were overbuilt for the neighborhood. A buyer finally came our way, and we were elated! We had already found the house we wanted to buy and felt certain God had promised it to us. It was vacant and owned by friends of ours. They allowed us to start painting in the house while we waited on our buyer's loan process. I excitedly worked on our new house, so grateful for the extra space it offered and the peacefulness of living on a quiet, dead-end street. Things were going smooth, and it looked like we were finally going to get out of that little house.

Then the dreaded phone call came one morning. The caller said that our buyer was not going to be able to purchase the house. I put the receiver back on its hook and paced around the house in aggravation and disappointment. While I was still trying to process the bad news, the phone rang again. I had just purchased a carload of beautiful red poinsettias for the Hanging of the Greens program at our church. I was the director of the program, in charge of the decorations, and had plans to go decorate the church that afternoon. The phone call was from my pastor, who asked if I'd purchased real or fake poinsettias. When I told him I bought real poinsettias, I was instructed to return them all and exchange them for fake poinsettias since we had a member who was allergic to the real ones. I knew about the member's allergies, but since she didn't live in our town and hadn't attended our church in several months, I made a decision to get the prettier, real ones. So I hung up the phone a second time with a mood that was quickly escalating into volcanic proportions.

There I was, alone in my little house, irritated with two separate situations. I felt as though I'd been sucker-punched. First, I got news that dashed all my hopes of ever getting to move out of my little-bitty home. Second, I was told to exchange twenty beautiful, large, red, real poinsettias for scrawny, ugly, fake ones. Besides the fake ones not being the best decorative choice, I was going to have to unload them all from my car and drag them to the customer service desk at Walmart. Oh, and did I mention that these phone calls came on the Friday after Thanksgiving, the busiest shopping day of the year? My morning had turned into a nightmare. My house deal fell through, and I felt unappreciated when told to change the decorations in my program! Let me just say, I was not a happy camper that day. I had just failed tests in both contentment and submission to authority.

Deep inside my heart, I believed God had promised us the house on the quiet, dead-end street. If I were to be completely honest, my anger that morning was directed mostly toward God. I pointed the blame at him since I believed he was in control of the whole situation. So I sat down on my couch—in my cramped, little living room—and proceeded to let my raw emotion flow out in prayer as I talked to God about anger, disappointment, and hurt feelings. With my Bible on my lap, I whined, complained, and pleaded my case to God. I figured there was no sense in hiding how I felt because he knew what was in my heart anyway. After a few minutes of crying this selfish and infantile type of prayer, my attitude changed. I decided to surrender to God's will. I remember sighing and telling the Lord, "If it's your will for us to live in this cracker box for the rest of our lives, not only will I do it, but I'll like it!" So, there, I did it. I relinquished what I wanted and committed to whatever the Lord wanted for us. I promised to be content in my circumstance, according to Philippians chapter 4. I would learn to be content. When my prayer was over, I didn't feel happy, but I felt satisfied. I trusted God to do what was best for my family. After I dried my tears and blew my nose, I opened my Bible and asked God to speak to me through his Word. I wanted and needed some reassurance and encouragement from him. My Bible fell open to the book of Deuteronomy chapter 1. I probably rolled my eyes, and I remember sarcastically thinking, *Well, that's just great. I doubt that there's a word for me in Deuteronomy!* That shows you just where my faith was that day—up one minute and down the next. Man oh man, was I ever wrong about the book of Deuteronomy. I looked down, and these verses jumped off the page for my eyes to read:

> The Lord our God spoke to us in Horeb, saying: "You have dwelt long enough at this mountain." "See, I have set the land before you; go in and possess the land."
>
> Deuteronomy 1:6, 8

My heart started pounding. It had run the gamut of emotions that day. I went from despair to surrender to excitement. God answered my prayer, and he was speaking to me now! He did promise us that other house and he would give it to us in his timing. I began thanking God for his goodness to me in reassuring me that he did keep his promises. I got up from my couch—in my cramped, cracker box of a little living room—and I went about my day with a spring in my step. I exchanged those poinsettias, decorated at the church, then went to our promised house and did more work there. I knew it was going to be our house someday. By the way, our friends had assured us they would hold the house for us until we sold ours. The morning those two aggravating phone calls came, prayer didn't change my circumstances, but it did change my attitude—and my level of contentment.

When Buddy came home from work that evening, I explained to him my rough morning, God's Word to me, and my new attitude. As we sat down to supper, Buddy explained his plan to the kids and me. He said we were going to pray every night at supper and ask the Lord to let us move into our new house by March 1. We began our prayer the weekend after Thanksgiving. I had faith and fully believed God would come through for us—until the middle of February. At that point, I had lost all hope of moving by March 1. A typical house purchase requires thirty days to complete the process. Time was up; we were about fifteen days away from March 1, and I was preparing for another disappointment. But God is faithful even when we are not—and even in the midst of our lack of faith. The morning of February 20, a Realtor called and brought potential buyers to see our home. They looked, left, and I barely got my hopes up. We'd had plenty of lookers before. About three hours later, the Realtor called back and said the potential buyers wanted to look again. That was a good sign! I wondered if it could really happen this time. When the people came back for a second look, the husband stopped and gazed a while out of the kitchen window. Then he turned around, leaned back on the counter, and said, "Well, I think we'll take it. It's gonna be a cash deal. We're in a hurry to move, so how soon do you think you folks could be out?"

While I picked my jaw up off the floor, Buddy jokingly replied, "How about midnight tonight!"

While giving glory to God and telling anyone who would listen of our testimony, we had most of our things moved into our new home by March 1! What a faithful Father we have! Our children witnessed his faithfulness as they prayed each night at supper and personally witnessed God in action on their behalf in answer to their prayers.

We settled into our new house and were content living there for several years. God then led us to sell that home and move ten miles away to save Buddy driving time to work. We searched the area with a Realtor but couldn't seem to find a house that suited our needs. Of course, we were looking for one that fit into our budget, but we also required a big indoor living space and ample parking for our family. I love to host our extended family events, and we have a very large family. At the time we were house hunting, we needed room to park thirteen cars, and that only counted my parents, three sisters, and their families. When aunts, uncles, and cousins came, which was most of the time, we needed much more parking space. Most of the homes we looked at were in nice neighborhoods with limited street parking. While our search continued, we rented a storage building and moved into an apartment, hoping it would be temporary.

We moved into a nice, clean apartment during the early summer months. Buddy and I found that we actually enjoyed it since we had a nice water view and had so few chores to do as compared to owning a home. I had a lot less to clean, and he didn't have any yard work to do. As nice as that was, we still didn't want to live there long, so we continued to search for the home that God wanted us to have.

I was content living in the apartment until the mouse invasion. I can't stand the thought of a mouse in the house. After we caught the first one, we reset traps, thinking it was just for good measure, and much to my dismay, kept catching them! We discovered that the nice lady next door was pouring birdfeed on the patio to attract the birds, but instead she was attracting mice! And somehow the little critters found their way right into our apartment. I wanted to move—right now!

Even after the mouse entry hole was found and sealed, my contentment in living there was gone. I was paranoid all the time, thinking another mouse was lurking just around a corner or maybe crawling on my pots and pans in the kitchen. I wanted to find a house and move out of there. But nothing in the real estate market seemed to fit our needs. If we liked the house, there wasn't enough parking. If there was enough parking, we didn't like the house. And there were always houses that met our desires, but they were out of our price range. It was about to become the summer of my discontent—or was it?

When I felt the walls closing in on me again and my emotions starting to spiral out of control, I had another little heart-to-heart conversation with the Lord about it. For the second time in my life, I made a decision to be content where I lived. I remember telling the Lord how bad I wanted to find a house and move, but that if he wanted us to remain in the apartment for a while, I would be content with it. Once again—like Paul said in Philippians—I had learned to be content. So the house hunt continued, but not with the same pressure and intensity that I'd had when I was frantically trying to get out of mouse central.

Shortly after I bent my knee to the contentment issue, my sister Kim called me. She was excited and said, "Hey! I've found your house!" She had just driven past a home on her way to work, and it had a new "for sale by owner" sign in the front lawn. She gave me the location, and I planned to go check it out right away. Before I had time to leave the apartment, her husband, Donnie, called me and said, "Hey! I've found your house!" He had noticed the same house that Kim did. I laughed and told him I was on my way there now.

When I pulled into the driveway of the house for sale, I chuckled to myself at God's sense of humor. Just a few weeks earlier, Buddy and I had looked at another house for sale in that same neighborhood. We weren't interested in that home, but when we drove past the house where my car was now parked, Buddy said, "Wow, wouldn't you like to live in that house?" The sale price was posted in big red letters on the "for sale" sign, so I knew right away we could afford this house. I knocked on the door and was met by a brother and a sister who appeared to be in their late sixties. The house had belonged to their parents, and since both had passed away, the house was now for sale. As they gave me a tour, I couldn't help but notice that this house had everything we had asked God for. With just under twenty-five hundred square feet, the house was big enough to entertain our family, and right beside the house was a parking lot that belonged to the church across the street. The house was in superb condition for its age, and I thought the 1950s art deco architecture was neat. I left there believing I had finally found our new house.

Buddy toured the house that evening. He loved it and wanted to make an offer but found out that another couple had signed a contract on it right after I'd left that day. This was a Saturday evening, and Buddy asked the homeowner if he would call us first if something fell through with the first offer. We went home, and I felt like the rug had been pulled out from under us but clung to my lesson on contentment. If this wasn't the house God wanted us to have, then I'd wait for the one he had for us.

Monday afternoon, Buddy got the phone call we'd hoped for. The house was ours if we wanted it. We wrote a contract that evening on a legal pad, and within thirty days we owned it. It has been a dream home for us. It has been a great house for entertaining, and there's plenty of room to park all our family cars. When I get to heaven, I'll be curious to find out if we would have ever gotten this home had I not learned to be content with the very first one.

> Let your conduct be without covetousness, and be content with such things as you have.
>
> Hebrews 13:5

We lived in our first little house for about seventeen years. During most of those years, I was not content, or thankful, for my home. In my eyes, it wasn't big enough, nice enough, and the neighborhood wasn't good enough. I always found something to complain about.

God used the homes I lived in to help me learn contentment. I came to a place where I was satisfied with what I had and even joyfully prayed, "Your will be done, Lord, not mine." I had to learn through this trial that I could trust God to control my life. I had to make a mental decision, which did not come easy, to allow him to decide where I would live. I discovered that once I relinquished that control to God, he provided abundant peace in my mind and spirit. I found freedom in not being in control. I found contentment with what I had. It was a long, hard lesson for me to learn, but it has brought me to a higher level of trust in God. And isn't that where God wants his children to eventually arrive? It's a place where they can trust him—regardless of their circumstances—and find that he has a better plan for them than they had ever imagined. He does give us exceedingly and abundantly above all that we can even imagine! We just need to seek him first, and all these things—even houses—are added to us. Oh, how thankful I am for learning to be content with what I have—and where I live.

TRIAL TEN: WHEN I AM REJECTED, JESUS IS MY ALL IN ALL

If it is possible, as much as depends on you, live peaceably with all men. Beloved, do not avenge yourselves, but rather give place to wrath; for it is written, "Vengeance is Mine, I will repay," says the Lord. "Therefore if your enemy hungers, feed him; if he thirsts, give him a drink; for in so doing you will heap coals of fire on his head." Do not be overcome by evil, but overcome evil with good.

Romans 12:18–21

Some of the most painful trials of my life have been those that included conflict with friends and loved ones. Each one of those conflicts provided the potential for me to receive deep scars of rejection. I must respect the privacy of those involved and not share the nature and details of those struggles. However, the impact those trials have made on my life—and my ever-developing character—is far too important not to mention it.

I want everybody to like me and have a strong tendency toward people pleasing. When I find out someone doesn't like me, it's heartbreaking for me. I take it very personally, and it requires a mental effort for me to fight off feelings of rejection and depression. I'm reminded of one conflict I had with a particular group of people. While serving as chairwoman on a committee fraught with inner divisions, I took an unpopular stand on an issue, and it resulted in me becoming the topic of gossip and ill feelings.

During the time of this trial, our church was hosting a revival. I was sitting in that revival meeting dwelling on the pain and irritation of being rejected and talked about. I had tried so hard to bring people together to work for our common cause, but I had failed in my effort to bring unity to this group. I believed there just had to be something I could do to bring this group into harmony. While I was praying and asking God what to do next, I heard the revival speaker say, "There's a woman here, and God has a message for you: 'You can't fix it!'" I knew immediately that that word was for me. I'd always been a slow learner in this area, thinking I could fix everything and everyone, but that was my turning point in realizing that people and their issues were God's problems to fix, not mine! All my efforts at trying to do God's job would be in vain. Like a lot of women, I'm a fixer, and I believed that if everyone would just cooperate with me, I could make everything all better. But God showed me that the truth of the matter is that he must do a work in all of us and we must cooperate with him if we are to ever dwell in peace with each other. It won't happen any other way. The farther people are from God in their daily walk with him, the farther they will be from one another. I realized at this point that what I perceived was a personal rejection against me was likely not the source of the conflict. The conflict simply revealed that our entire group, including me, had room for improvement in our daily spiritual walks with Jesus.

I found myself involved in another conflict when God moved us away from people in whom we'd given many years of our service, friendship, and love. I never dreamed these people would not be a part of our lives. Events came to pass, and after a great deal of prayer seeking God's will, Buddy and I both felt led to go a direction that took us away from our friends. It was extremely painful. Some of our friends understood and sympathized with our situation. Others criticized us behind our backs and accused us of not being in God's will. Some even perceived our decision as a personal assault against them and spoke strong words against us. It was a challenge to remain Christlike in the ordeal, and I wish I could say we succeeded in doing so. It was a sad, sad time for our family.

When I look at the situation from the backside of it, I clearly see several reasons why God had to move us away. Of those many reasons, I only feel at liberty to share the one that concerned my relationship with this group—and God. After the separation from our friends, I was finally able to see that I had been so busy working for God in this group that it interfered in my relationship with him. God pulled me away from people who depended on me and pulled me to a place where I depended on him. This pulling away transformed a time of grief to a time of excitement as I rediscovered my first love—God himself! I had been dangerously close—perhaps I was already there—to becoming like the church at Ephesus, which did all the right things but had left its first love. Oh, how thankful I am that the grace of God took me down that painful path of separation because that's where my first love stood waiting for me with open arms. With my focus back on him—where it had always belonged—he rekindled in me the flaming kind of love I'd once had for him. Safe I was in his arms, no matter who had rejected me or what awful things had been said about me. In my busyness of serving him, I had unintentionally left him. When he pulled me away from the distraction of service—as much pain as it brought me—I rediscovered that he was all I needed. I didn't need people or their approval. I needed him. He was my all in all.

I've also had conflicts with people I could describe as enemies. These were people who crossed my path and never had my best interest at heart and in some cases seemed anxious to intentionally inflict pain and ruin relationships. In most of those stressful conflicts, I simply severed relationships or broke ties so as to not deal with the enemy any longer. Basically, I just ran away from the enemy! As God continues to grow me up, I've learned that running away from the enemy is not always the right approach. Sometimes we must set proper boundaries to prevent future conflict, and that is certainly appropriate. But Jesus told us to love and pray for our enemies. In most of my conflicts, I could drum up enough spirituality to pray for my enemies—I just made certain I never had to be around my enemies again.

In the middle of one battle with an enemy, my rationale regarding an approach to an enemy changed. I didn't want to run away from this one. This was a battle over something that was precious to me, and I was determined to win at all costs. I was going to have to find a way to fight back—scripturally, of course. I had been attacked in a surprise assault by an enemy, and I was considering my options for a counterattack that wouldn't break a commandment—so murder was not an option! I was seething in the heat of this battle, and I had my face set like flint that I would not give up any ground to this enemy. But before I could plan my own tactic of offense against the enemy, God opened my eyes to a truth from the book of Jonah.

After Jonah was spit up out of the belly of the big fish, he obeyed God and went to the city of Nineveh. God had instructed him to preach to the people of this wicked city—who were the enemies of Jonah's people. When the people of Nineveh repented, God was merciful and did not bring disaster on them as Jonah had preached.

This made Jonah quite angry, and he went out of the city to sit and watch what would happen to Nineveh. I think that he was secretly hoping God would change his mind and destroy the city—just my imaginative guess. While Jonah was sitting in the scorching heat of this desert country, God made a plant to grow up quickly to give Jonah shade. As Jonah enjoyed a reprieve from the sweltering sun, God sent a worm to eat up the plant and a violent wind that surely stirred up the dust and sand. Once again, Jonah was exposed to the elements in the desert, where he grew faint in body and spirit. He was irate that the protective plant had died and left him uncomfortable.

> But the Lord said, "You have had pity on the plant for which you have not labored, nor made it grow, which came up in a night and perished in a night. And should I not pity Nineveh, that great city, in which are more than one hundred and twenty thousand persons who cannot discern between their right hand and their left, and also much livestock?"
>
> Jonah 4:10–11

Here's what the Lord taught me from this passage of Scripture: Jonah had received all the benefits of growing up in a nation that knew Jehovah as the one true God. In contrast, the people of Nineveh were pagan worshipers and practiced all types of sin. By no means was their sin excused, but they had not experienced the spiritual advantage of knowing God since childhood, as Jonah had.

God loved the Ninevites and wanted to have a relationship with them. God used Jonah as the vehicle to introduce himself to this wicked people. God's ultimate purpose toward the Ninevites was accomplished when they sincerely repented. God's ultimate purpose in Jonah is left untold since the book of Jonah ends with the verse above. When God provided the sheltering plant for Jonah and then took it away from him, perhaps he was trying to show Jonah the wickedness in his own pouting heart. Jonah cared more for a green plant and his own comfort than he did for the souls of his enemies.

We're left to wonder if Jonah ever repented of his hard-hearted attitude toward his enemies.

I studied this story while under attack from my own enemy. While reading it, God pointed out to me that I, much like Jonah, had been given advantages since my childhood that my enemy had never received. I had been raised in a home where I was given much love and affirmation. I had a healthy marriage consisting not only of love, but of mutual respect and friendship as well. I had learned to comprehend and apply the grace of God in my life and not live in bondage to legalistic works. When I realized that the person attacking me had never experienced any of these, my heart was suddenly full of love and compassion for such a wounded soul. In a single moment, God gave me a heart of flesh toward that person. God let me see just a little glimpse of how he saw my enemy, and suddenly the word *enemy* didn't describe how I felt about that individual any longer. Now, please understand that I didn't call that person and schedule a lunch date, but my entire outlook toward that person was changed. I still had to maintain a safe and healthy boundary to avoid future conflict, but I don't see this one as my enemy any longer. Like Jonah, God revealed to me my own wicked attitude and provided the grace to change my heart. Oh, friends, be thankful when God uses an enemy to foster in you Christlike compassion for others, as well as the ability to see where wicked attitudes lurk in your own heart.

> For it is not an enemy who reproaches me; then I could bear it. Nor is it one who hates me who has magnified himself against me; then I could hide from him. But it was you, a man my equal, my companion and my acquaintance. We took sweet counsel together, and walked to the house of God in the throng.
>
> Psalm 55:12–14

I've also been through trials where rejection and betrayal blindsided me because they came from the most unexpected of people at the most unexpected of times. These were gut-wrenching, tear-filled times. I never knew such pain could be caused by ones I loved so dearly. Only the love of God—and my sweet, supportive husband—got me through those bleak, awful days. But the shock and pain of these hurtful rejections were turned for good, as they also eventually brought a time of spiritual enlightenment to me. As I languished in the despair of feeling like my heart had been pulled out and stepped on, the Lord took my broken heart and put it back together so it would more closely resemble his own heart. I had planned on putting up emotional walls of protection so that no one could ever hurt me like that again. But instead, Jesus gently reminded me that he also knew the pain of rejection; he understood exactly how I felt. If I were to be more Christlike, I would have to learn to endure rejection—like Christ did.

> Then He said to them, "My soul is exceedingly sorrowful, even to death. Stay here and watch with Me." He went a little farther and fell on His face, and prayed, saying, "O my Father, if it is possible, let this cup pass from Me; nevertheless, not as I will, but as You will." Then He came to the disciples and found them asleep, and said to Peter, "What, could you not watch with Me one hour?"
>
> Matthew 26:38–40

Try to put yourself in Jesus' sandals as he prayed late one night in the quiet garden of Gethsemane. He knew the time had come to complete his earthly mission. He knew what anguish awaited him in just a few short hours. The strain of knowing what he was about to endure caused his flesh to sweat drops of blood—indicative of monumental stress. While Jesus agonized in prayer to his Father, not one of his disciple friends stayed awake and prayed for him. He was about to lay down his life for not only them, but also for the ones who were about to beat him unmercifully and crucify him. He faced the apprehension of it all without any human support. Later, at his trial, not one earthly friend openly stood with him. Jesus faced complete and undeserved rejection from his friends,; after all he'd done for them. He had daily given himself to them for three years, and then he offered his innocent life for them. And no one stood with him. His human heart surely started to break that night in the garden of Gethsemane.

The extent to which Jesus' heart was broken is beyond what you and I can ever comprehend or experience. He faced the ultimate in rejection. So, dear one, if your heart is breaking from the pain of rejection from those you love, just know that Jesus himself understands more than you know. Even as a child, Jesus probably experienced rejection because of the gossip surrounding the events of his virgin birth. During his three-year ministry, we read that his own hometown rejected him, and we know that the religious leaders of the day rejected him as well. Even some in his own family refused to believe in his deity until after his death and resurrection. Jesus faced rejection from different people from birth to death. Even when hanging on that cruel cross, with his life's blood pouring out of his precious body, with the sin of the world and a guilty verdict placed upon his sinless flesh, it appeared that his own holy, heavenly Father had also left him alone in his suffering.

> And about the ninth hour Jesus cried out with a loud voice, saying, "Eli, Eli, lama sabachthani?" that is, "My God, My God, why have You forsaken Me?"
>
> Matthew 27:46

The Bible tells us in 2 Corinthians 5:21 that the sinless Jesus became sin for us so we might be the righteousness of God in him. Sin separates us from the Father, and at the moment that Jesus became sin, the just Father had to judge that sin—and Jesus bore that judgment for us. Jesus' blood was shed for the remission of our sin. I do not understand all the intricacies of Jesus' crying out to his Father about being forsaken. Some argue whether or not God did forsake Jesus. I suppose we'll understand more when we get to heaven. But to help establish my point, we know that at least Jesus felt forsaken while he hung on that cross. But, thankfully, it wasn't long before Jesus could tell his Father that he committed his spirit into his hands. I don't know how long Jesus felt forsaken while he hung on that cross, but how dreadful it must have been for him.

How could Jesus bear such suffering and feelings of rejection? Because he had an inexhaustible love that kept him going. He went through this horrific ordeal knowing that there would be those who would refuse to accept his loving sacrifice. Yet he gave himself anyway. When I think about the times I have felt betrayed or rejected, it's only natural to also remember the sacrifices I made for those people. I have to ask myself, "Did I give and sacrifice for my loved ones expecting something in return?" The answer is, "No, I gave of myself because I love them." So in those cases, if I am to fulfill Jesus' commandment of loving as he loved, then I cannot allow my hurt feelings to exhaust my love for them. If I had never felt the pain of having my heart ripped out by someone I loved so much, then I wouldn't be able to identify with Christ in that area—although there is absolutely no comparison to the level of pain that Christ bore. But in my own suffering, I found that the inexhaustible love of God was available to me, both to receive from him and to give to others. This isn't anything I'm capable of producing within my own flesh, but it's a gift given by the grace of God to anyone willing to be used as his vessel. This love of God is unconditional and inexhaustible.

Still, bear in mind that it is perfectly in order to set boundaries with difficult and caustic people as they are needed. There are even rare situations when relationships may need to be severed. These are times when we must listen carefully to and follow the leading of the Holy Spirit. But even in those most difficult circumstances, by the grace of God, we can still exhibit the inexhaustible love of God to everyone he brings across our path.

The good result—and perhaps the end intended—of facing rejection from people is that it can force us into the arms of Jesus. The Andrae Crouch song "Through It All" speaks to that topic in reminding us that a time of loneliness can be transformed by the presence of Jesus.

In those lonely hours, yes, those precious lonely hours, Jesus let me know that I was His own.

—Andrae Crouch

Doesn't it just bless your heart to see that when life hands us heartache, Jesus hands us himself. Jesus knows better than any person on earth the pain of rejection, and he will stand with us when no one else will. Read what Oswald Chambers wrote on this same subject.

A servant of God must stand so very much alone that he never realizes he is alone. In the early stages of the Christian life, disappointments will come—people who used to be lights will flicker out, and those who used to stand with us will turn away. We have to get so used to it that we will not even realize we are standing alone. Paul said, "No one stood with me, but all forsook me … But the Lord stood with me and strengthened me" (2 Timothy 4:16–17). We must build our faith not on fading lights but on the Light that never fails. When "important" individuals go away we are sad, until we see that they are meant to go, so that only one thing is left for us to do—to look into the face of God for ourselves.

—Oswald Chambers

No matter what we face here on earth, it will never come close to the sorrow and pain Jesus endured as he loved and laid down his life for the very ones who openly rejected him. Our rejection trials pale in comparison and suddenly appear so petty and small. But still, Jesus has compassion for our hurt feelings, broken hearts, and troubled minds, and he stands with us—to strengthen us.

When you feel as if the whole world has abandoned you, Jesus is standing beside you. When you've been attacked by the enemy, Jesus is standing beside you. When you feel as though you've been betrayed and you're afraid to risk loving anyone else, Jesus is still standing beside you. When you think you can't face living without that one important person in your life anymore, look to Jesus—he is standing with you and he will strengthen you.

We must keep our spiritual eyes and ears open and search for things to learn and things to be thankful for in the middle of any conflict. When our closest friends reject us, we must look to Jesus, who wants to fill the gaping holes left in our hearts. Oh, how thankful I am for the pain brought by conflict, betrayal, and rejection, for it revealed to me that Jesus understood how I felt and stood beside me to strengthen me. What more could a lonely, rejected, and betrayed person ask for? He was, is, and always shall be my all in all. Praise his name!

CONCLUSION

Does the plowman keep plowing all day to sow? Does he keep turning his soil and breaking the clods? When he has leveled its surface, does he not sow the black cummin and scatter the cummin, plant the wheat in rows, the barley in the appointed place, and the spelt in its place? For He instructs him in right judgment, His God teaches him. For the black cummin is not threshed with a threshing sledge, nor is a cartwheel rolled over the cummin; but the black cumin is beaten out with a stick, and the cummin with a rod. Bread flour must be ground; therefore he does not thresh it forever, break it with his cartwheel, or crush it with his horsemen. This also comes from the Lord of hosts, Who is wonderful in counsel and excellent in guidance.

Isaiah 28:24–29

When a farmer begins breaking up his field in the spring, it's not for the sake of breaking up the field; it's for the intended purpose of bringing forth a harvest. Different crops require different methods of harvest, which can be violent, but they all produce food in the end. In the same way, I believe that God has allowed similar violent trials in my life as a form of threshing. I can see that it was a necessary process to reach the end God intended for my life. I expect more threshing in my life but am reassured to know that the threshing, beating, and grinding don't last forever. They serve their purpose of producing a harvest, according to God's will, and I'm thankful for it.

Giving thanks always for all things to God the Father in the name
of our Lord Jesus Christ...

Ephesians 5:20

I pray that the Lord has touched your heart as you've read through
the pages of this book. It is by no means an exhaustive book on
thanksgiving or trials, as I'm sure volumes more could be written
on this subject. I'm just an ordinary homemaker who felt led by the
Lord to share her thoughts on trials and thanksgiving based on her
own life experiences and the Word of God. You may have noticed
that many of the Scripture references are from the book of Psalms.
When you find yourself in a trial, I encourage you to read the Psalms
and let them soothe your mind, bring peace to your heart, and take
you to your knees in worship and thanksgiving.

My hope and prayer is that this book will be ointment to the
soul wounded by trial and that it will remind us all to give thanks
always for all things.

BIBLIOGRAPHY

INTRODUCTION

Crouch, Andrae. "My Tribute." Newbury Park, CA: Lexicon Music, Light Records, 1971.

Crouch, Andrae. "Through It All." Burbank, CA: Manna Music, Light Records, 1971.

WHY ME, LORD?

Strong, James. *Strong's Exhaustive Concordance of the Bible.* Nashville, TN: Crusade Bible Publishers, Inc. Page 57 of Greek Dictionary.

The NIV Study Bible. Barker, Kenneth, editor. Grand Rapids, MI: Zondervan Publishing House, 1984. Page 1880.

The Wycliffe Bible Commentary. Pfeiffer, Charles F., Harrison, Everett F., editors. Fourth printing. Nashville, TN: The Southwestern Company 1968. Page 1431.

Renner, Rick. *Sparkling Gems from the Greek.* 11th printing. Tulsa, OK: Teach All Nations, 2003. Page 345.

Renner, Rick. *Sparkling Gems from the Greek.* 11th printing. Tulsa, OK: Teach All Nations, 2003. Page 834.

Renner, Rick. *Sparkling Gems from the Greek.* 11th printing. Tulsa, OK: Teach All Nations, 2003. Page 601.

The Wycliffe Bible Commentary. Pfeiffer, Charles F., Harrison, Everett F., editors. Fourth printing. Nashville, TN: The Southwestern Company 1968. Page 1451.

Chambers, Oswald. *My Utmost for His Highest, Special Updated Edition.* Reimann, James. Grand Rapids, MI: Discovery House Publishers, 1995. Devotional page for April 4.

Chambers, Oswald. *My Utmost for His Highest, Special Updated Edition.* Reimann, James. Grand Rapids, MI: Discovery House Publishers, 1995. Devotional page for June 13.

Chambers, Oswald. *My Utmost for His Highest, Special Updated Edition.* Reimann, James. Grand Rapids, MI: Discovery House Publishers, 1995. Devotional page for June 8.

Chambers, Oswald. *My Utmost for His Highest, Special Updated Edition.* Reimann, James. Grand Rapids, MI: Discovery House Publishers, 1995. Devotional page for January 22.

Chambers, Oswald. *My Utmost for His Highest, Special Updated Edition.* Reimann, James. Grand Rapids, MI: Discovery House Publishers, 1995. Devotional page for April 27.

Strong, James. *Strong's Exhaustive Concordance of the Bible.* Nashville, TN: Crusade Bible Publishers, Inc. Page 39 of Hebrew and Chaldee Dictionary.

IS YOUR PATH GOOD OR BAD?

EVTV1, LLC. *Hee Haw* comedy skit, *That's Good, That's Bad.* Jaffer, Ali CEO EVTV1. Tinley Park, IL: 2009. <http://www.evtv1.com/>

Breakthrough with Rod Parsley. TV show.

Elliot, Elisabeth. *Through Gates of Splendor.* 1st Edition. New York, NY: Harper and Brothers, 1957.

End of the Spear. Every Tribe Entertainment. Green, Mart, CEO. Studio City, CA: 2005.

THE SCIENCE OF GRATITUDE

Emmons, Robert A.; McCullough, Michael E.; "Counting Blessings versus Burdens: An Experimental Investigation of Gratitude and Subjective Well-Being in Daily Life." *The Journal of Personality and Social Psychology* 2006, Vol. 84, No.2. 377–389. Copyright 2003 by the American Psychological Association, Inc. 0022–3514/03/$12.00 DOI: 10.1037/0022–3514.84.2.377.

Strong, James. *Strong's Exhaustive Concordance of the Bible.* Nashville, TN: Crusade Bible Publishers, Inc. Page 119 of Hebrew and Chaldee Dictionary.

Barium Blues. Editor Lydia Mancini. 2007. Article by Emoto, Dr.; "Water Crystals: The Power of Love and Gratitude Made Visible."*<http://www.bariumblues.com/conscious_water_crystals.html/>*

The NIV Study Bible. Barker, Kenneth, editor. Grand Rapids, MI: Zondervan Publishing House 1984. Page 1571.

The Wycliffe Bible Commentary. Pfeiffer, Charles F., Harrison, Everett F., editors. Fourth printing. Nashville, TN: The Southwestern Company 1968. Page 1056.

BE THANKFUL, EVEN IN TRIALS

"The University of Texas M.D. Anderson Cancer Center: Making Cancer History." "A Conversation with a Living Legend." M. D. Anderson Cancer Center luncheon held in Dallas. Printed in University of Texas M. D. Anderson Cancer Center newsletter. <http://*www.cancerwise.org/*January_2003>

TRIAL ONE: IGNORING THE SPIRIT

Chambers, Oswald. *My Utmost for His Highest, Special Updated Edition.* Reimann, James. Grand Rapids, MI: Discovery House Publishers, 1995. Devotional page for November 14.

TRIAL TWO: SCARED TO LIFE

Brumley, Albert E. "He Set Me Free." Stamps-Baxter Music, 1939.

TRIAL THREE: "GOD, I'M SO MAD AT YOU!"

Chambers, Oswald. *My Utmost for His Highest, Special Updated Edition.* Reimann, James. Grand Rapids, MI: Discovery House Publishers, 1995. Devotional page for April 20.

TRIAL SEVEN: ANOTHER DAY, ANOTHER JOB

The NIV Study Bible. Barker, Kenneth, editor. Grand Rapids, MI: Zondervan Publishing House 1984. Page 1892.

TRIAL EIGHT: "MOMMA, I NEED HELP"

Chambers, Oswald. *My Utmost for His Highest, Special Updated Edition.* Reimann, James. Grand Rapids, MI: Discovery House Publishers, 1995. Devotional page for May 15.

Chambers, Oswald. *My Utmost for His Highest, Special Updated Edition.* Reimann, James. Grand Rapids, MI: Discovery House Publishers, 1995. Devotional page for August 12.

Chambers, Oswald. *My Utmost for His Highest, Special Updated Edition.* Reimann, James. Grand Rapids, MI: Discovery House Publishers, 1995. Devotional page for May 3.

TRIAL TEN: WHEN I AM REJECTED, JESUS IS MY ALL IN ALL

Crouch, Andrae. "Through It All." Burbank CA: Manna Music, Light Records, 1971.

Chambers, Oswald. *My Utmost for His Highest, Special Updated Edition.* Reimann, James. Grand Rapids, MI: Discovery House Publishers, 1995. Devotional page for April 22.